PHILOSOPHER PICKETT

FIRST PAGE OF THE FLUMGUDGEON GAZETTE

Philosopher Pickett

The Life and Writings of Charles Edward
Pickett, Esq., of Virginia, Who Came Over-
land to the Pacific Coast in 1842-43 and for
Forty Years Waged War with Pen and Pam-
phlet against All Manner of Public Abuses
in Oregon and California; Including also
Unpublished Letters Written by Him from
Yerba Buena at the Time of the Conquest of
California by the United States in 1846-47

LAWRENCE CLARK POWELL

UNIVERSITY OF CALIFORNIA PRESS

BERKELEY AND LOS ANGELES · 1942

UNIVERSITY OF CALIFORNIA PRESS
BERKELEY, CALIFORNIA

CAMBRIDGE UNIVERSITY PRESS
LONDON, ENGLAND

TO MY WIFE
FAY

Poor old Philosopher Pickett passed quietly through the "gate" into another world where ends his earthly career, which no doubt has been one of more than ordinary interest were it written up by someone familiar with his history.—MARIPOSA GAZETTE, *November 18, 1882*

PREFACE

CHARLES E. PICKETT ... came to California in 1846. He was later known as "Philosopher Pickett," and was an able but greatly eccentric character. He wrote many pamphlets, and, from whichever point of view they may be regarded, their deeply radical nature cannot fail to engross the interested reader.

THIS NOTE by Robert Ernest Cowan in his *Bibliography of the History of California* first drew my attention to the subject of this study. I read several of Pickett's pamphlets and became engrossed. When I sought information about his career, I found that he had passed nearly into oblivion; apart from the sentences in Bancroft's "Pioneer Register," the only sketch of his life (numbering but a few pages) appeared in 1901, and since then only an occasional and incidental footnote has kept his name alive.

Passing curiosity was transformed gradually into a determination to resurrect this man. I found that in his time he had been one of the best-known men on the Pacific Coast, albeit as an eccentric, and that he was one of the most colorful figures in the history of the West. For forty years he had been in the midst of the events which had changed the West from wilderness to civilization. He took part in the provisional government of Oregon; he was at Sutter's Fort just after the Bear Flag Revolt, and in Yerba Buena when the American flag was first raised. He voyaged to the Sandwich Islands, whence he imported the first wool-bearing sheep into California.

As a journalist in Oregon he issued, in manuscript form, the first newspaper on the Pacific Coast, and later he edited a printed newspaper in San Francisco. A man whose passion was political science, he found himself living in one of the most corrupt eras in the history of our nation. By his rash and vehement manner of attacking the abuses which flourished in his time, he became known as a "crackpot"; but before he died, he saw many of the reforms he advocated adopted by the State in its new constitution of 1879. As a pamphleteer he possessed a fluent and forceful style. For years his was almost a lone voice of protest against the corruption which characterized the ruthless exploitation and development of California. He might be called the West's first reformer.

His life was no success story, cut from exotic cloth of gold. He was put in jail three different times, and lived most of his days in near poverty. Nor was he a crusading Galahad. He had his frailties. Frustrated ambition to become a power in the government made him all the more bitter against the dishonest legislators and judges, speculators and capitalists, who controlled California.

I have attempted to present the man as he was, in relation to the historical events with which, although he did not play a decisive role, he was closely associated. If he was no hero, neither was he a fool. Throughout a chaotic life he kept his integrity.

He never weakened or sold out. Pickett was a hot-headed Virginia gentleman caught up in the mael-strom of westward expansion and the discovery of gold; though cast aside repeatedly, he never went under. I have tried to bring out the logic of his character and development, and have set down only what I know to be true by virtue of historical docu-mentation.

In addition to the story of Pickett's life, I have included eight unpublished letters written by him from Yerba Buena and San Jose, relating to the con-quest of California by the Americans. These form a spirited and sharply critical commentary on the men and events of that decisive period in Califor-nia's history. His satirical account of the "Battle" of Santa Clara is probably the best ever written of that unsanguinary *opéra bouffe* event. To these let-ters I have added a biographical repertory of the per-sons mentioned in them.

In my search for material relating to Pickett, I have incurred numerous debts to my fellow librar-ians, to other workers in the field of western history, and to my friends. It is a pleasure to acknowledge them. To my chief, John Edward Goodwin, Librar-ian of the University of California, Los Angeles, I am grateful for his kindness in enabling me to secure photostats of those pamphlets by Pickett not in the library of that institution. The intelligent and un-tiring reference service rendered by the California

State Library proved invaluable; to its Librarian, Miss Mabel R. Gillis, and especially to its California section librarian, Miss Caroline Wenzel, I express heartfelt thanks. Likewise to the Director of the Bancroft Library, Herbert Ingram Priestley, and his staff, this study owes much. The friendly and informal atmosphere of that place makes it a joy to study there. Jens Nyholm, Assistant Librarian of the University of California, Berkeley, shared home and automobile with me while I was working at the Bancroft; *skaal* to him! Leslie Edgar Bliss, Librarian of the Huntington Library, and his staff, gave me every assistance by letter and in person; and to the Trustees of that institution I acknowledge permission to reprint the four Pickett letters in the Huntington's Fort Sutter Papers. Miss Dorothy M. Huggins, Secretary of the California Historical Society, and Mrs. Dolores W. Bryant, of the Society of California Pioneers, were helpful. In Honolulu, my former classmate, Willard Wilson, Assistant Professor of English in the University of Hawaii, delved into that port's archives to confirm the date of Pickett's voyage there. In Oregon, Miss Katherine Anderson, Reference Librarian of the Library Association of Portland, unearthed and worked over a rich cache of Pickett material in the Oregon Historical Society collections; and the Society's Librarian, Miss Nellie B. Pipes, was equally kind in providing me with photostats. To Earl R. Swem, Librarian of the Virginia State Library, and to the reference divisions of the Library of Congress, the National Archives, the New York Public Library, the American Antiquarian Society, the University of Washington Library, and the San Diego Public Library I am indebted for prompt attention to my queries.

Henry R. Wagner of San Marino encouraged me at all stages of my work and took up the search (alas, unsuccessful) for a picture of Pickett; and it was he who first suggested reprinting the Yerba Buena letters in full. To Robert Ernest Cowan I am grateful for much aid, and for his generosity in allowing me to reprint the Pickett letters from his private collection, which came into his hands directly from the original recipient, William Heath Davis.

William B. Rice, of the editorial staff of the *Pacific Historical Review*, located valuable data on Pickett as a journalist.

Miss Catherine Wilson rendered me great service in skillfully typing my notes and final manuscript.

William Everson of Selma drove me to Mariposa, where we searched in vain for Pickett's grave. My thanks go to him and his wife Edwa for their hospitality.

John Walton Caughey, Associate Professor of History in the University of California, Los Angeles, generously gave me the benefit of his experience in the writing of western history by critically reading the manuscript.

Credit is due Harold A. Small, Editor of the University of California Press, for painstaking and sensitive editing of the manuscript.

Lastly, to my wife I am grateful for annotating collateral works, for helpful suggestions toward the understanding of the Philosopher's character, and most of all, for her mere presence, which is the greatest incentive to work I have ever known.

L. C. P.

The University Library
University of California
Los Angeles

CONTENTS

ILLUSTRATIONS

I

The Picketts of Fauquier

THE PICKETTS of Fauquier County, Virginia, were one of the original southern colonial families. The accepted tradition is that three Huguenot brothers came to America in the seventeenth century, one settling in New England, another in the Carolinas, and the third in Virginia. From the Virginian, George Pickett, who can be traced back to 1680, descended the Picketts of Fauquier. They were of the proud landed gentry, staunch Episcopalians with some Presbyterians thrown in, and they were represented by hardy fighters in the Revolution, the War of 1812, the Mexican War, and at Gettysburg, where General George E. Pickett led the charge that is remembered by his name.

Charles Edward Pickett, a cousin of the Confederate general, was the ninth born (1820) of twelve children of Captain James Sanford Pickett and Nancy Smith Pickett. His father, who lived from 1768 to 1852, was the owner of Fruit Farm in Loudoun County, which adjoins Fauquier County on the north and in turn is bounded on the north by

Maryland. There Charles was brought up in the plantation tradition as a well-to-do farmer's son. He was educated at a near-by church academy not far from Mount Vernon, where he was thoroughly grounded in the classics, English literature, French history, logic, and rhetoric. His boyhood hero was naturally George Washington, and to Mount Vernon he made frequent pilgrimages. Later, his hero was Andrew Jackson, and Pickett at seventeen heard the President's farewell address read from the eastern portico of the Capitol, on March 4, 1837. This proximity to the nation's capital and its historic shrine seems to have imparted to the boy a marked sense of national pride.

He enjoyed the usual social recreations of the landed gentry, and attended at least one gala ball in Washington, where he waltzed with a boyhood sweetheart.

Late in his teens, when his academy course was completed (it was then 1839), young Pickett set out in the world on the first leg of a journey that was to take him as far west as the Hawaiian Islands. His bachelor brother, William Sanford Pickett, ten years older than he, was prospering as a commission merchant over the mountains in Memphis, Tennessee, and Charles went to live with him. The governor of Tennessee was at that time James K. Polk, who a few years later was to become the fourteenth President of the United States. Through his brother, Charles met the Governor, and gave him an allegiance that was to last until the latter's death in 1849. Polk was already preaching expansion and annexation, a philosophy that fired young Pickett to even greater nationalistic dreams than he had had when worshiping at Washington's shrine. The struggle of the United States and Great Britain for Oregon had turned everyone's eyes to the West. Many were going there, from motives both patriotic and pecuniary; in addition to a vigorous waving of the Stars and Stripes, the government was offering the prospect of free tracts of virgin wilderness.

Probably Charles was employed in William's commission house, but certainly such regular employment would have palled on him. Moreover, the elder brother married in January, 1842. When the official propaganda to colonize Oregon grew more intense, the fiery, restless young Charles had good reasons to pull up his stakes and head west. It was not long after his brother's marriage that he set out for the Missouri frontier, which was the jumping-off point for the Far West. His travel accessories included a bundle of clothing, two or three hundred dollars, and a copy of Lord Byron's poems. Henceforth this stripling Pickett, who was never to outgrow entirely the grandiose thoughts of idealistic youth, was to pursue for half a century the star of western expansion and conquest, and to play a quixotic role in many of the decisive events of Pacific Coast history.

2

The Plains and the Rockies

IN THE summer of 1842, Pickett, aged twenty-two, arrived in St. Louis, a chip on the tide of western migration, with his eyes on distant Oregon, where land was free and a new government was to be formed that would save the land from the British. He was brimful of the Democratic philosophy of "manifest destiny," and spoiling for adventure. He got it. A rogue named Charles Warfield, who was engaged in an intrigue for the Texan Republic against Mexico, took him in tow. Warfield's plan was to raise one hundred and fifty mountain men and capture the outgoing caravan of merchandise from Missouri to Santa Fé and Chihuahua, and the incoming one of specie, each represented as a prize of a million dollars. Warfield and his band were to retain half the spoils and turn the other half into the Texan treasury. The government of Texas had given him a colonel's commission and empowered him to raise troops for making the captures and otherwise harrying the Mexicans. Inasmuch as the Texan treasury was empty, Warfield was to provide his own expenses.

It was here that young Pickett, with his beltful of goldpieces and dreams of empire, proved useful. Warfield prevailed upon Pickett to buy him a horse, and from the American Fur Company he got a rifle and blankets; whereupon, accompanied by two other recruits, they set out westward over the great prairie. The meeting place was Bent's Fort, on the north bank of the Arkansas River, near Pueblo, Colorado. At this important rendezvous of Santa Fé traders and Rocky Mountain trappers they arrived on December 19, 1842, and settled down for the winter. Present as confederates were the Bent brothers, Kit Carson, Old Bill Williams, Ceran St. Vrain, and other hardbitten scouts, trappers, and plain rascals. What an adventure for young Pickett, who was fond of counting Norman raiders among his ancestors!

Alas for his dreams, the scheme met a serious setback when it was learned that Governor Armijo of New Mexico, having been informed of Warfield's rapacious plan, had organized a body of troops to guard the caravans to and from the crossing of the Arkansas. Most of the recruits withdrew, and Pickett turned his eyes again on Oregon.[1]

---

[1] Accompanied by a handful of men, Warfield persisted, however, and took the Taos trail to New Mexico, where he joined a larger Texan force under Jacob Snively. After several bloody encounters with Mexicans and Indians, in which the Texans came off best, the raiders were dispersed by a troop of United States cavalry for having trespassed on American territory. A participant's account of the expedition is found in Rufus B. Sage, *Rocky Mountain Life*, pp. 300 ff. For a list of contemporary references see Henry R. Wagner, *The Plains and the Rockies*, pp. 79–80.

By midsummer of 1843 he was at Bridger's Fort in Wyoming. At this squalid log camp on a tributary of the Green River he hobnobbed with James Bridger, talking with him about the topography and meteorology of the country and the feasibility of a transcontinental railroad. On August 14th he was swept along with the Oregon-bound caravan of nearly a thousand people, many from Tennessee and Missouri, led by Peter Burnett, William Martin, and Jesse Applegate. The arrival of this party in the Willamette Valley, in the autumn of 1843, more than doubled the population of the Oregon territory. The claim of the United States gained a strong reinforcement thereby.

In this nearly unbroken wilderness Pickett's politico-philosophical turn of mind developed rapidly, and manifested itself in a way that was to continue for the rest of his life. In their new home every man was required to build a house or help the community by other hard work, if in no other way than by hunting and bringing in game. Pickett would neither build, hunt, nor fish. He was a pioneer intellectual. His industry took the form of writing "pronunciamentos." The philosophy which he submitted for the government of the settlement was inscribed (for want of paper) on shingles, a product of honest toil which he so smoothed as to make them take the ink, and these he tacked to trees and posts in the most frequented places.

3

Alias "The Curltail Coon"

THE CENTER of political activity in the territory was
at Willamette Falls (later called Oregon City). In
that place, in the winter of 1842–43, there had been
organized the Pioneer Lyceum and Literary Club,
which met "to discuss the whole round of literary
and scientific pursuits." Gifted beyond his years with
both pen and tongue, Pickett was its secretary and
took active part in the debates. In later years pioneers
remembered the extraordinary range of Pickett's activity, from discussions that were sheer horseplay to
serious debates on the question of a transcontinental
railroad. The subject of government was dearest to
him. When, in March, 1844, a meeting of the American and Canadian settlers (sponsored perhaps by the
club) issued in French an address calling for coöpera-
tion between the two nationalities and objecting to
the continuance of a provisional government, the
document bore Pickett's signature as one of two
secretaries. Although Oregon historians attribute
authorship of the address to Father Langlois, a Canadian missionary, it appears that Pickett helped in

its composition; its sentiments and tone, especially in its remarks about law and lawyers, are also his.[1]

Life in the wilderness, even for an intellectual scribe, was no bed of roses. In the spring of 1844 Pickett fell ill and was taken in by the Reverend L. H. Judson, a missionary immigrant of 1838, and his wife, who gave him medicine and care. Later, when they sent him a bill for six dollars and upbraided him for what they declared to be his "abusive and hoggish manner and ungentlemanly conduct," the young Virginian fired a written blast at Judson that got a reply in kind. Unfortunately, Pickett's letter is gone; but Judson's has been preserved, and from it the following excerpts are taken:

Sir, your beautiful epistle has come to hand bearing date June 12, 1844. When first I perused that thing I was somewhat in a quandary whether I ought to take any notice of such a filthy and scurrilous article, and I called to mind the favorite maxim of Martin Luther, viz, "If you wrestle with a chimney sweep whether you throw or are thrown you will surely come off befouled." . . . I am most thoroughly convinced you can descend so low and use so much Billingsgate that I cannot render myself so mean as to meet you. . . . I have not charged you $3 for one dose of Calomel, but you know that in addition to that I gave you at your own request a sweat after the Thomsonian plan and attended upon you myself, and then at your own request spent nearly half a day in go-

---

[1] The document is reproduced in facsimile, with the French text and English translation, in the *Oregon Historical Quarterly*, XIII: 338–343.

ing up to the Mission school after an emetic, and after heating my water and preparing it, you refused to take it. For all the above and the attention of my family in waiting upon you, I have charged you only $3, and for nine days board (and I think you were there 12) only $3. . . . Notwithstanding your whining insinuations that you were not treated in a gentlemanly manner in my inhospitable house, that you expected that "the house of a missionary and a minister of the Gospel was a place where the stranger might have his wants supplied and the sick to be ministered unto without money and without price," yet I am bold to say that I always treat gentlemen as such, but he who comes to my house bearing the character of a spunge and a loafer and above all a debaucher with Indian women, I generally treat them as such, although sometimes I have treated such better than they deserve.[2]

Whether or not it was this retort vitriolic that routed Pickett, he quitted Oregon City for a trip to Astoria, the oldest settlement in the territory, at the mouth of the Columbia River. There he visited Colonel John McClure and J. M. Shively, the two original pioneers after the rise and fall of Astor's Fort. On July 1, 1844, the three were present at the arrival of the *Indefatigable,* the chartered vessel which brought to the Pacific Coast the first Catholic nuns to be transported hence, shepherded by the famous Father de Smet, who had made a journey to Belgium for missionary reinforcements. Pickett paddled out in a canoe and greeted the newcomers.

[2] Original in the Oregon Historical Society collections.

In contrast to his opinion of the Methodists, he found these Catholic immigrants "a highly educated and most excellent order of people." To those he liked Pickett gave enduring affection; and thirty-eight years later, when the surviving four of the six nuns were in charge of the Convent of Notre Dame in San Jose, California, he visited and corresponded with Sister Mary Catherine, the Superior.[3]

The following year, Pickett was back in Oregon City and commenced a feud with the Methodists. In this he was not alone; many of the newer settlers were protesting the excessive land claims of the missionaries. The richest part of the Willamette Valley was claimed as church property. Determined to break this monopoly, Pickett boldly staked off a homestead claim of one square mile on their vacant land at the junction of the Clackamas and Willamette rivers. Although he did not intend to homestead in Oregon, having decided to go to California, he could not leave without challenging the hated Methodists. Upon his 640 acres he built a cabin, planted grain, cabbages, and potatoes, made shingles, and lived alone on salmon, bread, potatoes, and "yerb"

[3] Pickett's memoir of the Astoria arrival, and a letter to him from Sister Mary Catherine, were later printed in a newspaper. An undated clipping from the *San Francisco Bulletin,* entitled "A Pioneer Reminiscential," *ca.* 1882, is in the California Historical Society collections; but a search of the files in the Bancroft and California State libraries has failed to place it exactly. A detailed account of the arrival is given in a letter written at the time by Sister Mary Aloysia, in C. E. Bagley, *Early Catholic Missions in Old Oregon,* II: 77–90.

tea. It was indeed a stubborn determination for social good that led him to the first manual labor of
his two-year stay in Oregon.

The church was unsuccessful in ousting Pickett,
even though it went so far as to incite the Indians to
attempt to murder him, and other land-hungry set-
lers then poured in and the missionaries' monopoly
was broken. The young intellectual had proved that
he could do more with his hands than merely push
a pen. Writing of this incident, J. W. Nesmith, who
had been a fellow traveler with Pickett in 1843 and
who eventually became one of the most influential
men in Oregon, testified to Pickett's accomplish-
ment:

The cause of Zion did not occupy their undivided attention, considerable of which was devoted to the acquisition of things that perish. Each missionary claimed 640
acres of land individually, besides 36 sections claimed
and held by the church. This claim of a principality
outside of their regular donation claims, caused about
the first litigation in Oregon, between the Mission and
Charles E. Pickett, who, in 1845, located upon vacant
land near the mouth of the Clackamas, and the Mission
brought suit to oust him, in which, aided by all the lawyers in Oregon, they were unsuccessful.[4]

His case won, Pickett ceased from his strenuous
homesteading labor and returned to the life of an

[4] Oregon Pioneer Association, *Transactions,* Salem, 1881. Pickett's
account is found in his *Address to the California Legislature,* pp.
4–5, and is reprinted in *The Paris Exposition,* p. 15.

intellectual scribe. During the session of the provisional government's Legislative Committee in the summer of 1845, he commenced the first newspaper on the Pacific Coast. This was a biweekly manuscript sheet, which antedated by six months the coast's first printed paper, the *Oregon Spectator*. He called it the *Flumgudgeon Gazette and Bumble Bee Budget*, subtitled "A Newspaper of the Salmagundi Order, Devoted to Scratching and Stinging the Follies of the Times." In place of his own name as editor, Pickett used the pseudonym "The Curltail Coon." He transcribed some twelve copies of each issue.[5]

Only a single number of this extraordinary paper is to be found today, in the Oregon Historical Society's library. It is Volume 1, Number 8, dated August 20, 1845—the day of the adjournment of the Legislative Committee. Its contents are for the most part satirical thrusts at the legislators. There is a conversation with a Tillicum Indian in which Pickett shows some knowledge of the Chinook jargon; a defense of Lewis and Clark and an attack on Vancouver; ridicule of the Legislative Committee's "big

[5] In later reminiscences Pickett proudly asserted his role in this venture; cf. *Western American*, February 17, 1852, and *Paris Exposition*, p. 10; also the present writer's article on the unique surviving issue, and transcription of it, in the *Oregon Historical Quarterly*, June, 1940. Hudson's *Journalism in the United States from 1690 to 1872*, pp. 590–591, credits the *Flumgudgeon* with being the first newspaper on the Pacific Coast. It quotes in full Pickett's account from the *Western American*. Hudson does not, however, mention Pickett by name, and seems not to have been aware that the *Flumgudgeon* was a manuscript newspaper.

brass gun"; a plea that more respect be shown to the local judges in court; and a reference to Pickett's latest feud.

This feud was with one of the most powerful and hated men in the territory, Dr. Elijah White, an immigrant of 1837 who had returned east and reappeared in Oregon in the fall of 1842, bearing a commission from the United States government as subagent for the Indians west of the Rocky Mountains. Pickett had differed with him in the Lyceum debates, in the course of which White had not concealed his ambition to become governor of Oregon. At this session of the Legislative Committee the doctor had became embroiled with its members, and Pickett seized the opportunity to lambaste him in the *Flumgudgeon Gazette*. He did not confine himself to a local campaign against the Indian agent. Aware of the value of his acquaintanceship with Governor Polk of Tennessee, now President Polk, Pickett sent copies of his paper and subsequent legislative proceedings against White to the President.

White was a shrewd foe, however, as the records show. There have been preserved by the Oregon Historical Society certain affidavits bearing upon the quarrel. The canny doctor intercepted a courier-borne dispatch to the East, and later deposed that he found therein "a packet of letters which were written by Mr. Pickett to different persons in the U. S., one of them to the Hon. President Polk, another to Mr. Pickett's mother, and I thought it my duty as an officer of the Government of the U. S. and bearing letters to a principal man in that Government to know what those letters contained, and on examining the letter addressed to President Polk, I found myself basely slandered by Mr. Pickett, tho' it was artfully written, yet it accused me of being a liar and a rascal."

With both Pickett and the committee against him, Dr. White went down to defeat. Their communications arrived in Washington before he did, and instead of reappointing him as Indian agent, President Polk tendered the appointment to Pickett. However, by the time the news finally reached Oregon, Pickett had left that territory for California.

After his experience in the role of the "Curltail Coon," Pickett was slated (according to his own account) to become editor of the *Oregon Spectator* when that newspaper made its first appearance in February, 1846, but a feud with the missionaries prevented this appointment. "A majority of the stockholders had fixed upon me to be its editor," he wrote in a later reminiscence, "but the Missionary Mercantile agent having imported the press, types and paper, and advanced money on them, refused to let the stockholders vote upon the selection of editor unless their lien should be first raised. As this was not done previous to my leaving Oregon, I was not permitted to mount the tripod."[6]

[6] *Paris Exposition*, p. 10.

As it was, Pickett had the distinction of placing in the first issue of the *Spectator* the initial real estate advertisement to appear in the West. He subdivided part of the claim which he had wrested from the Methodists. From the City Hotel in Oregon City he issued an invitation to prospective purchasers to inspect town lots at the foot of the Clackamas rapids.

Pickett's Oregon experiences included a short term on the woolsack. At the December, 1845, session of the Legislative Committee he was elected District Judge of Clackamas County in place of his friend Frederick Prigg, resigned. He was also one of the twenty-five original members of the territorial militia known as the Oregon Rangers.

In this same winter of 1845–46 his restlessness and love of change sent him on another wilderness adventure, this time with a party of five men to explore the country north of the Columbia as far as Puget Sound. Before reaching the mouth of the Columbia, they turned up the tributary Cowlitz River to its headwaters, and thence went overland on horseback to the Sound. In a borrowed canoe they paddled thirty miles up that body of water to the Hudson's Bay Company's establishment under the charge of Dr. W. F. Tolmie. There they were entertained for several days, and inspected the cultivated lands, and a sheep farm run by another Scotchman.

On the return voyage down the Cowlitz, Pickett stopped off at a settlement of French Canadians who

had begot, with the Indian women, numerous half-
breed progeny. There stood a Catholic church and
school administered by his old friend, Father Langlois, with whom he had collaborated on the Address
of 1844.

After many adventures and "hair-breadth 'scapes by
flood and field" (literally true, and not a mere poetical
quotation), I was invited by Father Langlois to spend
a week with him, he promising to send me with an Indian crew to Oregon City. Tired by working my passage,
and desiring to dry off after being soaked with rain and
swimming rivers through most of the journey, I gladly
accepted the invitation. After my party left, the reverend
father told me that he had practised a little ruse to de-
tain me; that his object was to gain time and opportunity to persuade me to remain there to teach English
to his scholars and better instruct him in that language,
offering in return to pay my expenses, instruct me in
the French language and make a Roman Catholic of me.
I told him that I would accede to his proposition, but
that I had resolved to start for California in the Spring.[7]

The question of the Oregon boundary, which with
that of Texas annexation had been a leading issue
in Polk's successful presidential campaign, was now
pressing for settlement. On the request of the Hudson's Bay people, Great Britain had sent the sloop-
of-war *Modeste* to anchor in the Columbia River
opposite Fort Vancouver. On his return from the
Cowlitz settlement Pickett boarded the sloop and
discussed the boundary question with the British.

---

[7] *San Francisco Examiner*, July 21, 1882.

Earlier he had written to President Polk, urging a compromise settlement with the English which would give them the entire island of Vancouver and set the 49th Parallel as a boundary. The British were demanding the more southerly boundary of the Columbia River. In June, 1846, the treaty of peaceful settlement between the two countries was signed. Not until early in 1847 did the news reach Oregon, and then it came by the devious route of Vera Cruz, Mazatlán, the Sandwich Islands, and the bark *Toulon*. To the end of his life Pickett liked to think that his firsthand reports to Polk and Buchanan had aided in the settlement. Perhaps they did. Certainly the terms coincided with his recommendations.

It was now the spring of 1846. Young Pickett had received no mail from home for several years. He had passed nearly three years in Oregon, and had vanquished such formidable adversaries as Dr. White and the Methodist missionaries. Journalism seemed to hold the most promising future for him, and yet the only newspaper in the territory was under the control of his enemies. And it came over him that he was homesick. It was going on ten years since he had left Fruit Farm in northern Virginia. His father, the captain, was now seventy-eight years old and would probably not live much longer, if he were living at all; and his mother was getting along in years. He determined to go home by way of California. A party was trekking overland through the mountains to Sutter's Fort. He would say goodbye to his friends, Prigg, Nesmith, and H. A. G. Lee, and go along south.

The news got around, and on May 23, 1846, there appeared before F. Prigg, who was again Justice of the Peace in and for Clackamas County, one Samuel Baker, who on oath deposed: "That Charles E. Pickett is justly indebted to one James Baker in the sum of Thirty dollars as per Bill filed, and I have every reason to believe that the said C. E. P. is about to remove from the County together with his property, and that unless a writ of attachment be issued against his effects, I shall be in danger of losing my just debt. Sworn. James Baker, X, his mark."[8]

A writ was issued. A jury found for the plaintiff in the sum of only three dollars. Pickett paid, and then bade farewell to Oregon.

---

[8] Original MS in the Oregon Historical Society collections.

4

Yerba Buena

THE TRAVELERS made their way through the mountains by way of Grant's Pass. In the Rogue River country they were successful in fighting off an attack by Indians. On June 4th they were camped on the bank of the Klamath River in northern California. Pickett, who made a hobby of collecting geological and mineral specimens, noted the presence of rocks rich in copper and iron, and remarked to his fellows that he thought gold in abundance would soon be found there.

In the diary kept by Sutter at his fort in New Helvetia the entry for Friday, June 26, 1846, reads, "Arrived an American man-of-war boat from the Yerba Buena, Lieut. Riviere and Dr. Henderson. Arrived a small party from Oregon (seven), Wood, Wornbough."[1] Writing of this entry, Bancroft says: "Chas. E. Pickett was probably one of these men. There were several small parties that came southward from Oregon, leaving but slight trace in the records beyond the names of a few members."[2]

[1] *New Helvetia Diary*, p. 44.   [2] *History of California*, V: 526.

Again Pickett arrived in the thick of things. The Bear Flag Revolt had taken place only ten days before, and at Sutter's Fort he found imprisoned Colonel Mariano Guadalupe Vallejo and his fellow Sonomans. As a result of orders by Frémont, the Californians were being harshly treated—kept in close confinement and allowed no communication with friends or families, and fed on coarse food. Vallejo was actually one of the most enlightened and far-seeing men in the land, and much in favor of the American acquisition of California. His imprisonment by the rash revolters was an act of stupidity. The young Virginia gentleman appreciated the injustice of the situation, and when he was pressed into serving as one of the guards over the prisoners, he gained Vallejo's lifelong friendship by his sympathy and kindness.[a]

Pickett made another friend at this time in Lieutenant Edward M. Kern, topographer and artist with the Frémont expedition, who had been placed in command of the fort, much to Sutter's disgust. Kern was a talented and well-bred young Philadelphian of Pickett's age, and the two found each other rare company in the howling wilderness of New Helvetia.

California was in a ferment. War with Mexico had been declared; the news had not yet reached the

---

[a] *Ibid.*, p. 125. Thirty years later, Pickett was urging the candidacy of Vallejo for electoral nomination; see his article in the *San Francisco Examiner,* July 20, 1876, and letter of the same date to Thompson, Huntington Library MS.

Coast, but was expected at any time. From Kern, Pickett learned of the presence of American naval vessels in the coastal waters, and, perhaps hoping for letters from home, he went down the river to Yerba Buena, arriving there early in July.[4]

Again he appeared on the scene at a decisive moment in history. On July 7th, Captain William Mervine, commander of the U. S. S. *Cyane* and U. S. S. *Savannah,* acting under orders from Commodore John D. Sloat, raised the American flag over the customhouse in Monterey, thus formally taking possession of California for the United States. Two days later, Captain John B. Montgomery, commanding the U. S. S. *Portsmouth,* performed the same ceremony in the plaza at Yerba Buena. Pickett was undoubtedly present at this stirring event.

Such decisive action was pleasing to Pickett, after the years of debate and litigation in Oregon. He made himself known to Captain Montgomery, certainly not neglecting to mention his acquaintance with President Polk. The alcaldeship, held under the Mexican regime by José Jesús Noë, was now vacant; and, according to Pickett, it was offered to him by Montgomery. For reasons unknown to us he declined it.[5] He did, however, perform scouting missions for Montgomery along the Contra Costa (the

---

[4] His name is included in the first directory of Yerba Buena, compiled by W. H. Davis as of July 9, 1846. See his *Seventy-five Years in California,* p. 377.

[5] *Paris Exposition,* p. 13.

eastern shore of San Francisco Bay), and reported to him on the question of pueblo land titles.

At this time the community by the Golden Gate was made up of three parts—the village of Yerba Buena, the presidio, and the Misión San Francisco de Asís—the total population of which was only several hundred people, mostly native Californians. Yerba Buena (which was not known as San Francisco until the following January) was the American settlement. In the very center of the village, on the edge of the bay, at No. 2 Montgomery Street, corner of Clay, stood the wooden store of William Heath Davis, merchant and trader, which had been built in 1838. Here Pickett made his home for the next two years.

If Montgomery had remained in Yerba Buena as commanding officer, things would probably have continued to go well for Pickett, for the former was highly regarded by all as a kind and conciliatory gentleman and an able executive. He was ordered to San Diego, however, and thence from Californian waters. His successor, Captain Joseph B. Hull, of the sloop-of-war *Warren,* was a man of smaller caliber. Davis describes him as "frequently in hot water, getting into various difficulties; inclined to be over particular and fussy . . . A man of small mind . . . unpopular with the people."[6]

Fresh from his Oregon triumphs and afire with nationalistic fervor, Pickett found Hull unsympathetic to his offers of service. A feud developed, and

---

[6] *Op. cit.,* p. 273.

when Hull heard of an offensive remark uttered by
Pickett, he used the power that was his by virtue of
the state of martial law and placed Pickett under
arrest. He ordered him to remain on the premises of
Davis' store as a prisoner of war, telling him that
should he go away from the store he would have
him confined in close quarters aboard the *Warren*.
Pickett was highly indignant, but thought it pru-
dent to comply.

The letters that Pickett wrote during this period
to his new friend Kern at Sutter's Fort and to Davis
while the trader was off down the coast in his brig
Euphemia show him to have been acutely aware of
all that was going on around him. They are important letters for the sharply critical picture they give
of the confused period of martial law, drawn by one
who was arrayed against those in power.[7] His sympathy was with the Californians who were aroused
by the lawless raids upon their livestock and property by the United States military authorities.

It was a maddening time and one which offended
Pickett's sense of justice and desire for law and order.
He was a member of the Yerba Buena Volunteers.
"The hardest service rendered," he wrote, "was in
standing guard, during the cold and rainy nights of
that dreary Winter, in the outskirts of the little vil-
lage of Yerba Buena, and scouting in the vicinity."[8]
He did not take part in the "Battle of Santa Clara,"

---

[7] See pp. 133 ff. below. [8] *Address to Veterans of Mexican War*, p. 2.

inasmuch as Davis was away at the time and Pickett was responsible for the business in his absence. The ticklishness of that winter season and the extreme nervousness of Hull and Mervine (which prompted Pickett to call them "grannies") are best indicated by John Henry Brown's anecdote of the coffee-pot bombardment:

The next thing that happened of any note, was the bursting of the coffee-pot in Brown's Hotel. Captain King, who arrived from the Islands, brought with him a newly patented coffee-pot, the like of which I had never seen before, nor since. It held about a gallon and a half. On the top was a large iron wheel, which fitted right to the tin; over that was a cover; on the outside was a screw, which could be turned with the fingers. It could be screwed down so tight that no steam could escape. Captain King had with him a Kanaka steward, who had learned how to use the coffee-pot with safety, and had done so several times. It was their habit to make coffee in this pot every day; but, it so happened at this time that the steward had other work to do, and after fixing the coffee-pot, as he supposed, all right, he left it in charge of the second cook, with instructions if too much steam escaped to turn the screw tighter; and the cook turned it down so tight, that no steam could escape. The consequence was that the coffee-pot exploded, blowing the cook twenty yards from the kitchen; also, scattering the cooking utensils in different parts of the room. At that time Captain Hull's head-quarters were on the north side of the hotel. When he heard the explosion he ran immediately to the Barracks, (which were in the old Custom-House), and ordered the long roll to be beat, as the Spaniards had come to take the city....

Captain Hull demanded the call of the citizens, who very promptly responded, and he ordered them to form in line, and be ready to fire at the word of command. He also sent out some marines, as scouts, to find out the strength of the Californians. He made signals for the men on ship to be ready, if required on shore.[9]

Throughout the autumn of 1846 Pickett quarreled with the military regime verbally and in correspondence. Yerba Buena was without a newspaper. The only journal in the state was the *Californian,* which had been founded in Monterey the previous April. Meanwhile, when the ship *Brooklyn* arrived in San Francisco Bay it had as part of its cargo one small Hoe hand press, brevier and minion types, and a paper supply estimated to last two years. The owner of this material was a printer from New York State, Samuel Brannan, whose twin purpose was to establish a Mormon colony and at the same time build up a newspaper business. After some sample printing in the autumn of 1846, S. Brannan, publisher, and E. P. Jones, editor, issued on January 9, 1847, Vol. 1, No. 1, of the weekly *California Star.*

This was a happy event for Pickett, and served as an outlet for the spleen accumulated during the winter. In this first issue of the *Star,* under the pseudonym "Yerba Buena," he caustically criticized the alcalde, Washington A. Bartlett, former lieutenant on the *Portsmouth,* accusing him of misappropriat-

---

[9] *Reminiscences and Incidents of Early Days in San Francisco, 1845–50,* pp. 58–59.

ing town funds and of failing to have a survey made. Pickett also scolded another village official for smoking in the courtroom. Bartlett called on Captain Hull for an investigation of Pickett's charges, which was made by a committee composed of Leidesdorff, Howard, and Guerrero, who exonerated the alcalde from any suspicion of having mismanaged the municipal receipts—which amounted to $747.

Soon after this setback, Pickett wrote to the newly appointed (by President Polk) civil governor, General Stephen W. Kearny, who had replaced Frémont, that the alcaldes throughout California were "but a mockery to law and justice, assuming and exercising prerogatives and powers far beyond any clothed [i.e., vested in] them by the Mexican or United States laws. One great cause of discontent is the course of the Navy in reference to property purchased or taken, and money obtained for government purchases. There has been a most ignorant and infamous proceeding in this business, and the whole country is now suffering much distress in consequence. Suspend these alcalde courts or define their limits."[10] In his letters to Kern and Davis Pickett gleefully recounted the thorny trouble he was causing Hull. When Jones of the *Star*, fearful of the suppression threatened by Hull, refused Pickett any further space in which to press the quarrel, Pickett turned savagely upon him.

[10] Bancroft Library, unbound document no. 147, p. 50.

Pickett did not lack sympathizers among his fellow Yerba Buenans; unfortunately most of them were young naval officers (some of them former schoolmates of his), who were by necessity compelled to remain silent; chief among these was the purser of the *Savannah*, Lieutenant Daingerfield Fauntleroy, crack marksman of the fleet, a Virginian and neighbor of Pickett's boyhood.

Pickett was a good enough tactician to assume a new pseudonym and take a different tack. Accordingly, a series of milder, more constructive letters began to appear in the *Star*, signed "Paisano."[11] They treated of the questions of electing representatives, apportioning government land to individuals, and adopting a code of laws to govern California—land and government, Pickett's favorite topics. More personal were two letters protesting the announcement that levies made by government forces on private individuals in the course of the Mexican conflict would not be repaid until appropriated by Congress, and protesting the inability of the Frémont volunteers to collect their pay. (Pickett later presented a claim for a rifle, $100, horses, $160, and saddle, $75, which went unpaid.)

What was Pickett's profession? Bancroft, Cowan, and other writers call him a lawyer. Their authority

[11] Josiah Royce said he had identified "Paisano" as Lansford W. Hastings, the lawyer and land promoter, but gave no proof of the identification. (*California*, p. 208.) Nor can I prove that the writer was Pickett.

seems to have been a card which appeared in the first two months' issues of the *Star:*

A CARD

C. E. Pickett, attorney at law, having located himself permanently in the town of Yerba Buena, will practice his Profession in all the courts of this Department, and, also act as agent for the collection of all debts intrusted to his care.

The fact is that Pickett, as he admitted later, was not a lawyer; and after the withdrawal of this card from the *Star,* he never claimed to be one. It is true that he was of a legalistic turn of mind; and, fresh from the judgeship of Clackamas County, he probably decided to cash in on what knowledge he did possess. This was a common practice in the days of the Gold Rush. As his letter to Davis shows, he was reading law at this time. In later San Francisco directories Pickett listed his occupation as "philosopher" or "journalist." In the 'sixties and 'seventies he had desk space in various lawyers' offices, and in the course of the years he acquired a fluent command of legal jargon and a hearty contempt for the devious workings of legal practitioners.

5

The Farthest West

THROUGHOUT his life Pickett had the good sense to go away for a change of scene when his immediate path became too crowded with obstacles. Hence, in the Northwest, his trips to Astoria and Puget Sound; and so it was in San Francisco, when he became temporarily sick of the confused state of affairs.

William Heath ("Kanaka") Davis, in whose store Pickett made his home, had close ties with the Sandwich Islands—where he had been born in 1822. When, on account of his mother's illness there in March, 1847, he prepared to sail for Honolulu in his brig, the *Euphemia,* Pickett prevailed upon him to take him along. They left on the 31st, in a southeast rainstorm, and for two days Pickett was sick, until the storm abated.

The *Euphemia,* under Captain Thomas Russom, was not much to look at. Davis regretfully admitted that she was like to a box or a tub, and that she was a slow sailer; but she carried more than double her tonnage in freight and proved a gold mine for her owner. On this voyage she was drawing nine feet of water, and carried in addition to her three passengers (a Miss Eliza Jane Vines was the third) a cargo of furs, shingles, tallow, and specie represented by twenty bags of Mexican dollars. After a voyage of nearly three weeks they sighted the brilliant green seamark of Diamond Head, and coasted safely into the harbor of Honolulu on a fair Sunday morning.

Pickett remained nearly four months in the Islands, during which time he was progressively disillusioned about the idyll he had anticipated. A reading of Melville's *Typee* had led him to expect a peaceful, innocent, contented, and joyous primitive society. Instead, he found that the missionaries had done their work of transformation—missionaries! a class he had thought to have seen the last of in Oregon—and created a "mercenary, dissolute, enslaved and priest-ridden population." On the 9th of August, after he had been there three months, he vented his disgust in a joint letter to his old friends Lee and Prigg in Oregon.

. . . God help the Christianized nations, for the missionaries here can't or rather they have not done it, as they are now worse in character and condition than before these holy modern apostles came amongst them. The fact is I have at last arrived at the conclusion I have been so long aiming to get to. That religions of all sort, and particularly the Christian, are wholly and totally false, obscene, fabulous, arrant humbug. But nowhere on the globe is such a farce made of the Jesus Christ order as at these islands. I don't believe there is a single Kanaka in the Pacific Ocean who believes in the doctrines they teach. . . . The character of the native population may be summed up in two words. They are all whores and rogues. Not an honest man or a virtuous woman amongst them, from the King and Queen down.[1]

Fortunately, Pickett did not dwell on this vexing state of affairs any longer than was necessary to relieve his spleen. He spent much time in nature study, speculating on the evolution of species and the geological age of the islands. For his cabinet of minerals he gathered exotic specimens. "I have some beautiful specimens from the nether world," he wrote Lee, "the extracted essence of hell, solidified and cooled, which I obtained boiling hot out of the top of one of the chimnies to Pluto's palace and fiery chaldron and furnace below—alias, some lava from the volcano of Kilauea on Hawaii."

While in the valley of Waimea on the island of Hawaii, he dispatched one of his characteristic newsy letters to Davis in near-by Honolulu. It is worth quoting in full:

I find I am constantly changing all my plans in travelling. Instead of remaining ten days at Maui after I wrote you, I left next day for Hilo, but getting sick of my sea travel stopped this side of the island, to go by land to Hilo and then to the volcano. But here again my course is turned, as I go directly on to the volcano and then to Hilo, where if no vessel be ready to sail soon for Lihaina, I shall return here in order to ascend Mauna Kea, and

[1] Original MS in Oregon Historical Society collections.

wait till an opportunity for going presents itself. This is the climate for you—thermometer now ranging from 60 to 70 in the course of the day—and a fine plain all around, with the open sea and snowy mountains to look upon. My health is getting fine—good appetite and mind as well as body bracing up.

I find there are no oranges or pineapples to send you yet, as they are not ripe about Hilo and none raised this side of the island.

The d——d Missionaries prohibit travelling on Sunday, and I was told that had I started directly for Hilo to morrow (Sunday) instead of the volcano as I do that my servant with my baggage would be stopped and I have to pay a dollar fine to go on. Can this indeed be the law?

I believe I mentioned to you the sum I wished placed at my disposal at Honolulu by you or Mr Grimes. I think $400 will answer me, and as you requested I may want but little of it in money as the bills I make may be settled through Mr Grimes house without. If you and he shall have left before my return, direct his clerk or agent in the matter, and so arrange it that what money I want of this sum I can get. Mr Reynolds at Lihaina has a small library I have bought and my bill for this and a few other little articles, will be with Punchan and Co. about $100. I will try and arrange this without calling for the money.

I told Mr Thompson to put the bureau I got of him aboard the Euphemia—see to this. Dont forget the sheep. Examine them or get a judge of wool to do it for you, or else Mr Bush may pull some of the article over your eyes in the purchase.[2]

---

[2] Original in the Davis Papers, California State Library.

This mention of sheep indicates a change in Pickett's thought. Politics had become distasteful to him. He had decided that upon his return to California he would devote himself to agriculture, horticulture, and stock raising. Born and reared in the country, he had been memorably impressed by his visit while in the Northwest to the Scotch farmer and sheep raiser on the banks of Puget Sound. It was Pickett himself who finally purchased the sheep—five young, nearly pure Merinos, two rams and three ewes—with the intention of introducing wool growing into California. After much difficulty he succeeded in getting them to Honolulu, where he guarded them with care and solicitude ("for occasionally they played truant into the streets") in the yard of his hotel for a month.

Late in August he took the sheep aboard the American schooner *Providence* and sailed for San Francisco. It was a long passage of thirty-five days, throughout which he cared for the creatures with complete devotion.

6

Sonoma

THE NEWS that greeted him on his arrival was that President Polk had appointed him Indian Agent for Oregon in place of the ousted Dr. White. In Oregon the announcement had been the occasion for a fierce attack upon him by his missionary foes. Pickett had laid himself open to this attack by writing, after his experience with the Indians on the trek from Oregon to Sutter's Fort, a letter to the *Oregon Spectator,* which said:

Treat the Indians along the road kindly, but trust them not. After you get to the Siskiyou Mountains, use your pleasure in spilling blood, but were I travelling with you, from this on to the first sight of the Sacramento Valley my only communication with these treacherous, cowardly, untamable rascals would be through my rifle. The character of their country precludes the idea of making peace with them, or ever maintaining treaties if made; so that philanthropy must be set aside in cases of necessity, while self-preservation here dictates these savages being killed off as soon as possible.[1]

Such words were hardly calculated to gain support for Pickett as Indian Agent, and his foes turned them

---

[1] April 29, 1847.

vigorously against him.[2] According to Pickett, in a
letter to Lee, some of the charges on which he was
arraigned included "being guilty of highway rob-
bery on the plains of Missouri! stealing salt-tongues!!
cheating a poor widow woman out of a jug of butter
to speculate on!!! picking up small things about a
house!!!! lying—but the Catalogue is rather lengthy
so I'll stop!"

Pickett was wise enough to recognize that there
was no going back. Oregon belonged to the past. He
wrote to President Polk and Governor Abernethy,
formally declining the appointment. And to Lee he
sent a personal explanation of his decision:

Having not the slightest idea of receiving an appointment to *any* office in Oregon, I left that country with
the full intent of going back *home,* as I never looked
upon or felt Oregon to be much. And though I took
California, as I intended taking other countries in my
route thither; yet it was my full determination to keep
on; and remained here three months and within a short
time of my intended departure, ere I finally concluded
to make it my home. 'Tis true my restless brain and
somewhat wild, impulsive and reckless nature, has given
me erratic habits; but California, being an open, extended, beautiful and variegated country, with abundance of game and variety of scenery, with which to feed
my excited fancy and give employment to roving pro-
pensities, I shall be able to *miltite*[3] here, and remain

[2] See "A. Q.'s" letter in the *Spectator,* September 2, 1847, to which
Pickett replied with characteristic vigor in the issue of February 24,
1848.

[3] A term Pickett acquired in the salmon country.

within the bounds of the territory—at least for some years.

Those three months of blue devils, and uncertainty about leaving, for which I had been longing—spent in Oregon City the gloomy winter preceding my departure, made such a deep impress on my memory, that the bare *idea* of going back, even to fill the highest office the President or people there may ever have it in their power to bestow, brings on such a fit of the horrors, that I am compelled immediately to take a draught of the ambrosial juice, extracted from the unsurpassed grapes of our sunny southern clime, in order to soothe my excited feelings, restore equanimity of temperament, and prevent a suicidal catastrophe. I shall smuggle you a few bottles another time. But don't let your rabid teetotalers know who sent it, or else it will be arrayed in the list of criminal charges against my character to be sent on to the President (if such has not already been done) to effect my removal from office.

This same letter to Lee, in which Pickett appears as one of the earliest specimens of the California booster, is the longest and most intimate of all the Pickett epistles that have survived the years. It is a fascinating potpourri of news, abuse, cosmic speculation, and quotidian observation. Friend Prigg is denounced for having failed to forward via the *Whiton* Pickett's mail from home. The Indian Agent appointment is disposed of. His Oregon City foes are damned as "vulgar, tinpeddling, shaving, picayune, upstart Yankee and Cockney canaille." The missionaries are flayed. An odd request is made of Lee to

send for Pickett and Kern ("one of the really intelligent, honorable, and high minded gentlemen I
have met with in California") four flattened Siwash
craniums, two Cluckemens and two Tillicums.[4] He
dwells on his new foes in California. ("Men here
have been bribed and incited to dishonesty, by reason of there not being a shadow of genuine law in
the land since our flag went up, and precious little
before that.") From there he goes to the subject of
taking a wife, perhaps a Castilian. ("There are a few
very sweet and handsome ones in the land; and besides other things I have a curiosity for crossing the
breed to see if it can't be improved. I am rather
choice in the selection of an article of this kind, having seen nothing in the shape of woman west of the
mountains yet, unless one of these, that I could think
of mating with, though she had the gold of Croesus
to back her other charms.") He then refers mysteri-
ously to an important task he has to perform during
the next year or two, and concludes with a characteristic account of the offices he has declined; remaining, "Your friendly fellow mortal in this fleeting
short-lived stage of our existence, C. E. Pickett."

Pickett then shipped his sheep by launch to Sonoma, and spent a month or two in San Francisco
seeking to raise as much money as possible with

---

[4] On February 10, 1847, Richard M. Kern wrote from Philadelphia to his brother Edward that Dr. S. G. Morton, the eminent
scientist and author of *Crania Americana*, desired Edward to pro-
cure Indian skulls for him.—Huntington Library MS FS 117.

which to commence his pastoral existence. From
W. A. Leidesdorff he received $25 for one sorrel
horse, and of Alcalde Hyde he asked a writ of execution to collect a judgment of $200 which the alcalde
had rendered in his favor against Robert T. Ridley.[5]
He also acquired a lot on North Beach. Then he followed his sheep up the bay to Sonoma.

He chose this locality probably because it was the
home of Vallejo, who, perhaps in gratitude for Pickett's kindness to him during his imprisonment after
the Bear Flag Revolt, had placed some land at Pickett's disposal. For the next six months Pickett lived
at Sonoma, in the tranquil calm before the storm
of gold. It was probably the happiest time of his
life. To James Douglas, chief factor of the Hudson's
Bay Company at Fort Vancouver in Oregon, he dispatched a box of grapevine cuttings, requesting in
return some apple, plum, gooseberry, raspberry, and
currant scions and bushes. He has left us a sketch of
a Sunday morning spent with Vallejo.

We had been playing billiards at the Beasley and Cooper
Hotel at that little burg, situated opposite the old
Mission buildings. On coming out we heard someone
preaching in the church. This being an unusual occur-
rence, I asked the General what it meant, suggesting
that we go in for curiosity. "Diablo!" he responded. "It
is that little Indian rascal, Santillan, and I would sooner
call the dogs and run him out of town." I stepped to the
door and looked in, when there was the little padre

---

[5] MSS in Bancroft Library.

preaching away to one solitary listener—old Berryessa—
and he so drunk as to lean against the wall for support,
it not being the custom then to have seats in these old
churches.[6]

To round out the good life, Pickett took up pen
as the Sonoma correspondent of the *California Star*.
This time his pseudonym was "Pacific." In keeping
with it, and with the pastoral setting, he started out
calmly enough. The issue of January 15, 1848, con-
tains two of his communications: the first is a jocular
letter, locating Sonoma on the map and telling of
a fandango he has attended; the second is a serious
epistle about the Indians of California as an inferior
race. (It should be recalled that Pickett was from a
slave state, reared on a plantation; he thus looked
upon the Indians as equivalent to the Negroes—a
slave race.)

Pickett soon warmed to his job, and in succeeding
issues he cast out the spirit of his pseudonym and
proceeded to flay the alcaldes and to lament the evil
rulers and call for an honest civil government. One
"Humanitas" replied, chiding him for his "inhu-
man" regard for the Indians, and for his dissatisfaction with existing conditions; whereupon "Pacific"
Pickett donned martyr's robes and wrote:

It matters but little to me at present, whether "Humanitas," or others in this land, choose to consider my writ-

[6] An undated clipping from the *San Francisco Bulletin*, entitled
"A Pioneer Reminiscential," *ca.* 1882, in the California Historical
Society collections.

ings as intended for "the mere gratification of coming down on the administrators of the law in this country," or not, as henceforth I cease any further efforts in the cause, as a profitless and thankless business—profitless I now find both to the country and myself; though the last is of secondary moment, as those aware of my having rejected offices, popularity, and the means of acquiring wealth, in order to pursue my own course, must admit.[7]

Of course he did not cease his "efforts in the cause." Throughout the spring of '48 he continued to write on the state of affairs in California, the Mexican conquest and further American expansion, and indulged in polemics with such correspondents as "Humanitas" and "Sober Second Thought." Gold had been discovered on January 24th, at Sutter's mill on the American River, but the rush had not yet started. In the *Star* of May 13th there appeared what was to be Pickett's last letter from Sonoma—a humorous description of a picnic in the fields. Two days later the shrewd Mormon, Sam Brannan, galloped his horse down the streets of San Francisco, holding aloft a flask of shining particles and roaring, "Gold! Gold! From the American River!"

The rush was on. Within two weeks San Francisco was almost deserted. The *Star* folded up. The California pastoral was ended forever.

---

[7] February 26, 1848.

7

Gold

ALAS FOR Pickett's plan to become a country squire!
By summertime Sonoma was deserted like the
rest of the coastal towns. Shepherds and gardeners
were all gone to the mines. His sheep strayed and
were devoured by the coyotes. His orchard of imported fruit trees and berry bushes burned up in
the fierce sun for lack of water. Pickett gave in and
joined the rush.

But he did not go as a miner. The *Star*, which was
revived on November 3d as the *California Star and
Californian* (having thus merged with Colton's original Monterey paper), carried the following advertisement.

SACRAMENTO STORE
C. E. PICKETT
dealer in
General Merchandise
New Helvetia, Sacramento
and
Colloma Saw Mill, American River

C. E. Pickett, having opened a store at Sutter's Fort,
offers for sale, dry goods, ready made clothing, blankets,
hats, caps, boots, shoes, wines, liquors, cordials, preserved meats, fruits, nuts, provisions, groceries, cooking

and mining utensils, cutlery, tobacco, cigars, snuff, etc. etc. Will also continue his trading post under charge of F. Hampton, at the Colloma saw mill, in the mountains, where the above mentioned articles will be sent as the market below furnishes a necessary supply and the wants of the miners in that vicinity require.

He had come to the fort as early as July. At the celebration on Independence Day, attended by Governor Mason and Captains Sherman and Folsom, Pickett was the orator of the day, and, according to Sutter, he did his part creditably.[1] He was not completely swept away by the rush; he still found time to take pen in hand. In the first reissue of the *Star* we find him again in the role of "Pacific": "I snatch a few moments from that eager and all absorbing pursuit in which the whole population of this land is at present engaged, *Governor and the rest of our Military State Officers included,* to offer some remarks on that same old question, 'Civil Organization in California.' " In a later issue he pointed out the shocking fact that even the Preachers had left their Pulpits to engage in the vulgar delving for gold. He also fired a few rounds at Captain Folsom, to which the former quartermaster replied heatedly: "Pickett has been known here for the last two years as a turbulent, discontented man, for the otherwise inexplicable eccentricities of whose conduct, his friends have apologized by calling him *insane.*"[2]

---

[1] Sutter's diary in *The Argonaut,* February 11, 1878.
[2] *California Star and Californian,* December 16, 1848.

How you described storekeeper Pickett, aged 28
years, depended on whether you were friend or foe.
A friend remembered him at this period as doing a
thriving business, and that "many individuals have
ascribed a good deal of eccentricity to Pickett; but
we only knew him as a talented, noble-hearted, magnanimous gentleman."[3]

In odd moments, when not engaged in trading or
writing letters, Pickett did manage to pan a little
gold. Along with the report on the Gold Rush—since
become a classic—which was sent to Washington by
Colonel Richard B. Mason (who acted for a time as
governor), and which started the stampede from the
East, a specimen of gold was included which had
been obtained from "C. E. Pickett, American Fork,
Columa."[4]

By the winter of 1848 Sutter's Fort was a mad
jam of traders and miners, each and all bent on
material gain. Sutter had rented every inch of space
within the enclosure. Pickett's store occupied part
of the northeast bastion, which included an enclosure where he kept some of the nonperishable supplies. Adjoining were the premises of a trader from
Oregon, one Isaac W. Alderman, known as "White
Horse." Alderman was a bad hombre, having killed
two men before leaving Oregon. When he claimed
the use of Pickett's enclosure, on which one of his

[3] Santiago's reminiscences of Sutter's Fort, *Alta California*, August 3, 1866.
   [4] 31st Cong., 1st sess., Ex. Doc. 17, 1850, pp. 528–536.

doors also opened, the alcalde decided the matter in favor of Pickett. Again Alderman trespassed, and again Pickett's rights were upheld. This time, Pickett nailed up Alderman's door from the outside, whereupon "White Horse" came into the enclosure and advanced on Pickett with an uplifted axe. The latter, being armed with a shotgun, retreated as far as the wall, warning Alderman not to come farther. Alderman only cursed and kept advancing. Up came the shotgun, and two barrels of buckshot knocked Alderman flat. Within half an hour he was dead.

Then ensued the first trial at Sutter's Fort. It was clearly a case of self-defense, but Alcalde Bates was a business partner of Alderman's and encouraged feeling against Pickett before prudently delegating authority to the second alcalde, Fowler. This official promptly resigned, as Pickett was dangerously aroused against what he regarded as an unjustified prosecution. Sam Brannan finally agreed to serve as alcalde. Bancroft has given us a sardonic account of the trial.

On being brought into court, which was held in a room on the western side of the fort, Pickett was requested to lay his arms on the table, which he did. On the same table stood a plentiful supply of brandy and a pitcher of water, of which judge, jury, prisoner, and spectators partook at pleasure during the trial; the brandy, from its rapid disappearance, being evidently more to their taste than the water. Then the question seriously arose whether in a criminal court, where a man was on trial for his life, smoking was proper. [The question was probably raised by Pickett himself.] Appetite presses a strong argument; precedent was found in the California women who smoked at bull-fights, executions, and funerals, and if ladies indulged in the practice, tobacco could not be out of place anywhere.

The trial proceeded; equity in its broadest forms alone was sought, but still there must be the form. At length the judge rose and began a plea for the prosecution. "Hold on Brannan" said Pickett, "you are the judge." "I know it," Brannan replied, "and I am prosecuting attorney too." Brannan the pleader then addressed Brannan the judge in conjunction with the jury; after which Pickett arose, tossed off a glass of brandy, and made a telling speech, for he was an able man. As soon as it was over, the night being well advanced, the jury scattered, more intent on finding their beds than a verdict. Then the question arose, "What shall be done with the prisoner?" "Place him in confinement," said the judge. "There is no prison," replied the sheriff. "Put him in irons." "Got none," said the officer of the law. Making a virtue of necessity the judge then called the ayes and noes, whether the prisoner should be admitted to bail. The ayes had it. The prisoner took from the table his revolver and bowie-knife, and marched off. Next day the jury were drummed together, held a conference, and disagreed. [Four were for acquittal, three for manslaughter, five for willful murder.] A new trial was ordered and the prisoner acquitted.[5]

---

[5] *California inter Pocula*, pp. 608–609. The latest biography of Sutter, by J. P. Zollinger, errs in stating that Pickett shot Alderman in cold blood. Bancroft called the act one of self-defense (*California inter Pocula*, p. 608); that Alderman's character was bad is plainly recorded in Bancroft, *History of Oregon*, I: 459; and the only actual eyewitness account of the shooting (W. R. Grimshaw's, in *History*

An amusing incident of the trial was provided by Captain Sutter, who was a member of the jury. One of the witnesses for Pickett was testifying to the bad character of Alderman, when Sutter woke up from a doze, listened attentively for a moment, then rose to his feet and said, "Gentlemen, the man is dead and has atoned for his faults, and I will not sit here and hear his character traduced." The captain, who was noted for his devotion to the little brown jug, then started to leave the courtroom, and was with difficulty persuaded to resume his seat.

Pickett and Sutter had been boon companions until the arrival of Sutter's son in the summer of 1848. The young Swiss found his father in a befuddled state and persuaded him, as a protective measure against his debtors, to sign over all his holdings to him. Then young Sutter, for some reason or other, rented Pickett's quarters to another tenant and compelled Pickett to move into an adjoining room. Pickett was furious. He berated young Sutter, without satisfaction. Then he instituted a civil action against Captain Sutter before Alcalde John Sinclair. The case was dismissed for lack of cause. Pickett stubbornly continued to insist that Sutter owed him for the loss he suffered. It was several years before the matter was finally settled.

---

of Sacramento County, pp. 124–125) states, "As the killing was manifestly in self-defense, the affair would have gone no further had it not been for the efforts of Sam Brannan." Burnett said, " . . . he killed a bad man named Alderman under very justifiable circumstances" (Recollections, I: 302).

As a trader Pickett was out of his element. His fellows were a razor-sharp, crafty, and shrewd lot of highbinders, as foolish Sutter found out when they were through with him. Pickett was too kindhearted to down-and-outers, too easygoing and ready to extend credit. By the autumn of 1849 he was in bad financial shape. He notified his debtors that their accounts must be voluntarily balanced by gold dust soon, or he would call on the aid of what shadow of law there was in the land to force settlement. He also threatened to publish the names of those debtors who did not pay up.[6]

Even so, this was the most prosperous period of his life. In addition to his trading posts, he acquired land in the new towns of Sacramento and Sutterville. Pickett took a prominent part in the movement to organize a government in California, and served in his old role of secretary of a corresponding committee. At a mass meeting of the citizens of the Sacramento district, assembled in Sacramento City on July 5, 1849, he was one of ten leading settlers nominated to attend a constitutional convention. In November he announced his candidacy for a seat in the State senate. He was not elected.[7]

By 1850 the flood of immigrants was nearly overwhelming. Hundreds of sick and indigent persons were stranded in the towns. Pickett's heart was touched by all the suffering he saw, and to a private

[6] *Placer Times,* September 29, October 13, 1849.
[7] *Placer Times,* June 30, July 7, November 3, 10, 1849.

hospital in Sacramento which was caring for the needy he stood as guarantor for a sum of nearly ten thousand dollars. When the hospital went bankrupt, Pickett was forced to pay its debts.

He was unfitted for the sharp practices which were making the fortunes of the Sam Brannans. Little by little his holdings melted away. In 1851 he liquidated his business activities and planned to return to San Francisco, with a few thousand salvaged dollars, to devote himself to his two true loves, political reform and journalism. The pastoral dream was gone beyond recovery, dispelled by the discovery of gold: "A discovery that has brought more evil, crime and deeply damning pollution upon this fair Western land, than had a hundred Pandora's boxes been opened in it."

"Indeed," wrote Pickett, "I hardly ever pillow my head at night without mourning over the contrast of what is and what would have been in California but for the curse the Almighty has sent upon the land. But for the infernal Gold, bringing with it an influx of the offscourings of all nations, the vile and vicious of every land and clime, and with its tainting touch and influence making men grossly selfish and knavish, who may have brought some virtue in them hither, we should have been able to boast of a country and an innocent, contented, joyous population, as would entitle it to be termed an hesperian Arcadia."[8]

---

[8] Letter in the *California Farmer*, March 20, 1857.

8

The "Western American"

SAN FRANCISCO in the early 1850's was the scene of a twin struggle: of the immigrants for land, and of the politicians for control of the State machinery and Federal patronage. Into both plunged Pickett. In 1851 he attended the meeting of the legislature in San Jose. This body attained a certain unique position in the State's history as the "Legislature of a Thousand Drinks." Pickett's way of describing it was more direct. "It is known to fame," he wrote, "for its venality and corruption beyond any legislative body that ever sat in Christendom."[1] And its members he called "an infamous, ignorant, drunken, rowdy, perjured and traitorous body of men'"[2]—a description which is quoted to this day by historians, although its source has been forgotten.

In the summer of 1851 Pickett announced the founding of his own newspaper, to be devoted to the cause of reform. On July 20th, from Sacramento City, he wrote to John Bidwell in Hamilton, California, enclosing copies of a prospectus. Apparently

---

[1] *John C. Frémont,* p. 11.   [2] *Western American,* January 27, 1852.

no copy of this announcement has survived, but Pickett's letter is among the Bidwell Papers in the California State Library. It reads in part:

I enclose you some copies of my prospectus. Put all but one in the hands of some active persons in your region in order to get me subscribers, and that keep yourself to fill up. There is going to be no failures in this affair provided men who know me will do what I ask in order to get a start, and this is but a small affair. Indeed I have a right to demand this aid of all who care a fig for the interest of California. We are in a dreadful state of turmoil and confusion, and things will continue to grow worse unless someone makes a start to stem the tide of corruption and rascality flooding the land.

Hanging a few Sidney Coves and greasers is going to do but little good, so long as men high in office are allowed to retain their posts, and continue practicing every species of fraud and villainy. We who wish to lead a quiet life in California and have a government based on proper principles—such a one as we can confide in and render a heartfelt support in upholding—must come out and denounce the present order of things and declare for a change. It is high time this was being commenced. There is a vast field of labor before us—a perfect Augean stable to be cleaned, and I am willing to be one of the first to commence the task.

Early the following year, Pickett was in San Francisco, ready with the aid of a group of "practical printers" to publish his newspaper and to serve as its editor. It was a daily called the *Western American*. The first issue appeared on January 15th, and carried an "Introductory Personal" in which Pickett declared himself "a disciple of Epicurus in philosophy, of Jesus Christ in morals, and of Thomas Jefferson in politics."[9] Pickett apparently sent copies of this first issue to other newspapers in the State, and on January 24th the *San Diego Herald* printed the following leg-pulling notice:

THE WESTERN AMERICAN

This new daily makes its appearance under the auspices of Chas. E. Pickett, Esq. Its object is to increase the already numerous moral, social, commercial and political virtues of the people of California. Though such an undertaking would seem to many both novel and desperate, we hope to see it entirely successful. By the introductions, we learn that the Western American is in favor of a new State Constitution, a division of the State, a permanent Capital, squatters' rights, pre-emption laws, mineral laws, the Pacific railroad, free trade, Louis Kossuth, Smith O'Brien, Epicurus, Jesus Christ, Jefferson, Jackson and Calhoun; and opposed to Cos-

[9] E. C. Kemble in the *Sacramento Union*, December 25, 1858. No copy of the first issue of Pickett's newspaper appears to have survived. In Vol. 130, pp. 697–698, of the Hayes Scrapbooks, Bancroft Library, are several clippings from the first issue, including the "Introductory Personal" and part of the original prospectus. There is no complete file in existence, and only two single issues are to be found in California, one in the Huntington Library, the other in the Pasadena Public Library. The New York Historical Society has seven issues, the Library of Congress twenty-five; it is from a microfilm of the latter file that my study has been made. Because of this scarcity of examples the story of the *Western American* until now has never been told, except in another version of this chapter by the present writer in the *Papers* of the Bibliographical Society of America, December, 1940.

sackdom and Sir Robert Walpole. With so many on his
favorable side, we hope he will find no difficulty in over-
coming all his opponents.

It was Monday the 26th before the second issue of
this "daily" appeared; thenceforth it continued reg-
ularly six days a week. An imposing list of agents was
printed, which included J. L. Menks and Jesse Applegate in Oregon, E. K. Woodward, St. Louis, J. W.
Hampton, Washington, D. C., Pickett's younger
brother Gustavus Adolphus in New Orleans, B. D.
Wilson in Los Angeles, and various men in the towns
of Auburn, Shasta City, Sonoma, Benicia, Sacramento City, and San Jose. The paper's office was on
Montgomery Street (which then was on the water-
front), near Pickett's old home in Davis' store, three
doors from Clay, opposite Page, Brown & Co.'s.

The front page of each issue was given over to a
printing of the San Francisco police ordinances, a
list of members of Congress, and congressional reports such as T. Butler King's on steam communication with the Sandwich Islands and China. Page two
was the editorial and news section, written almost
entirely by Pickett. Page three was made up of ad-
vertisements, and page four of State laws.

Short and stormy was the life of the *Western American*. Its rivals, the *Picayune, Herald,* and *Alta,* were
repeatedly flayed by Pickett, and he also went afield
to do battle with the *Stockton Journal* and *Sonora
Herald*. His crusade was for an equitable settlement

of land titles. He was also opposed to Vigilante action, and called for an enlargement of the San Francisco police force, which numbered only thirty men. In two weeks the circulation reached fifteen hundred daily. Copies of a weekly "steamer edition" (at 25 cents), the front page of which reprinted the past week's editorials were wrapped for mailing, to be sent to family and friends "back in the States."

The paper had its lighter moments. Pickett was no blue-nosed reformer. No one enjoyed good living more than he. Oysters were consumed in the office before closing time; the Jenny Lind Theater was scolded for not providing the *Western American* with passes; a *partie française* was inaugurated for French readers. And when Pickett took a day off to witness the marriage of his marine reporter, John B. Ward, to Señorita Arcadia Concepción Estudillo of San Leandro, the paper ribbed the absent editor, "Governor" Pickett, on his unmarried state. The following day he gave a lively account of his trip to the wedding on the good ship *Hector,* and printed a humorous resolution of thanks to the captain, crew, and bartender of the vessel.

On February 9th, Pickett announced to the legislature, then in its third session, his candidacy for the office of Public Printer. He refused, however, to send free copies of his newspaper to members of the legislature, even though he was a candidate. He said he was too poor; and besides, it would be bribery!

Pickett allied himself with the squatters, or set-
·tlers, against the land pirates and speculators. It was
no abstract quarrel; he had once been evicted as a
squatter. In the winter of 1846–47 he had fenced a
tract of land on Rincon Point (now Rincon Hill)
and erected a shack thereon. When he sailed for the
Islands he left his claim in the care of Eliab Grimes.
In his absence the military authorities claimed the
land, evicted Grimes, and destroyed the improvements. Upon his return, Pickett sought unsuccess-
fully to regain possession of the real estate; it had
passed into other hands. Thus it was natural for him
to embrace the squatters' cause and to lend his newspaper office for their meetings.

It was a losing battle. His little capital was nearly
gone, and advertising was increasingly hard to get.
He accused the *Herald* of trying to put him out of
business. His stock of newsprint was running low;
he began to advertise for "Printing Paper, 24 by 34
inches." And, as a final blow, he fell ill. The issue of
February 24th nevertheless sounded the clarion call
of "Reform! Reform!! Reform!!! Though stretched
upon a bed of sickness, our voice shall still be heard!"
But the next weekly edition lacked altogether his
fiery touch. The end came, for the newspaper, on
Monday, March 1, 1852, in this "Apology":

Colonel Pickett, the editor of this paper, is still confined
to his bed, and unable to furnish the readers of this
paper anything. He has now been ill for ten days, but

his medical attendants are of opinion that he will soon be restored, when the "W.A." will be conducted as heretofore. In the meantime our readers must bear with us until the Colonel is "himself again."

Although Pickett eventually rose from his sickbed, the *Western American* did not.

9

Pamphlets for the Times

EVIL DAYS had come upon Pickett. All his money had been sunk in the *Western American,* and to no avail. He remembered the sums he had advanced to pay for immigrant aid in the winter of 1849–50. Fortunately, he had kept all the accounts and vouchers relating to that business, and so to the third session of the legislature he presented a petition asking for reimbursement of the money he had spent. It was favorably received. "This gentleman," the report on it read, "is now greatly in want of the funds which he liberally advanced for the succor of his distressed countrymen. He was then in prosperous circumstances, but a reverse of fortune has fallen upon him."[1]

An Act for the Relief of Charles E. Pickett was passed, and approved by the governor. Pickett received $9500.[2] The *Western American* had been dead

---

[1] California Legislature, *Senate Journal,* 1852, p. 431.

[2] *Ibid.,* Doc. 5, Annual Report of the Treasurer, "General Fund Payments," p. 17. Frances Cahn in *Welfare Activities . . . in California, 1850–1934* (1936), p. 138, is mistaken in declaring that Pickett never received payment.

more than·a year when this good fortune came to him; there was no use in trying to revive it.

He had not forgotten his grievance against Sutter for having allowed his son to move him out of his preferred quarters at the fort in 1848. He conceived a sly plan of action. Drawing up a legal instrument which lacked only the signature of Captain Sutter, he went to Hock Farm for a visit. Sutter dispensed his usual brand of pioneer cheer, and for several days the two men quaffed from the flowing bowl. When Pickett left, he had Sutter's signature on the document, which read in part: "This is to certify that I have this day sold to Charles E. Pickett for value received and in full of all accounts and debts between us this day, all my right, title and interest now owned and held in the town of Sutter as originally surveyed, in a tract of land one-half mile fronting on the Sacramento River and extending back one mile." The bond, however, yielded Pickett no profit. Sutter did not have a single acre of unencumbered land in the Sacramento Valley.

For two years Pickett pressed his claim. Finally, in 1854, he took it to court. Sutter appeared in his own defense and said that, under duress, and to rid himself of a nuisance, he had signed Pickett's document. In the judge's instructions to the jury, they were informed that if the instrument was obtained while the defendant was under the influence of liquor, and if Pickett had any agency in Sutter's drinking for the purpose of obtaining said writing, it was thereby voided. The deliberation was brief. "We the jury," read the verdict, "find for the defendant." Sutter was discharged, and costs of $800 were assessed against Pickett. He appealed the case to the State supreme court, but this tribunal upheld the lower court.[3]

In 1855 he returned to San Francisco and took up the cudgel anew for squatters' rights. On June 16th he was one of several to address a settlers' meeting in Musical Hall. A few weeks later his speech was printed in pamphlet form, with additions, under the title, *A Pamphlet for the Times! containing an Address of C. E. Pickett to the Settlers of California, their Platform of Principles, and other matter, Showing the workings in this State of Broderick-Biglerism.* It was the first of the many pamphlets he was to issue in the course of the next twenty-five years.

In addition to the Tammany-bred politician Broderick and the tool Governor Bigler, the San Francisco banking house of Palmer, Cook and Company was attacked by Pickett. The following declaration of principles was set forth.

1. The passage and execution of a law that will amply protect the Settlers and miners in their improvements upon lands that have been, or may be, decided by the Courts to be the property of individuals.

---

[3] *Reports of Cases Argued and Determined in the Supreme Court . . . 1855,* pp. 412–413. The exhibits and transcript of the case are in the State archives in Sacramento. Cf. *Sacramento Bee,* December 30, 1939, "While an Empire Crumbled Away," by Harry P. Bagley.

2. The Homestead Law remaining as it is.

3. The exemption of miners' claims, to a reasonable extent, from forced sale on execution or otherwise.

4. The law regulating the occupation of the mineral lands remaining as it is.

5. A modification of the present Pre-Emption Law; making it protective without limitation, and extending it to all public lands in the State of California—save only the mineral lands—without reservation, on account of unlocated or imperfect grants.

Cleland has said of this first decade of state politics in California that a high level was never attained, and that "the people showed such little interest that political control passed almost entirely out of their keeping into the hands of a few skillful, energetic men, whose bitter rivalry for control of party machinery added an exciting, though unedifying, element to the otherwise monotonous course of local politics."[4]

Pickett was not one of the uninterested ones. No one at the time saw more clearly than he what was happening in California. The foundations of monopoly and exploitation, which stand even to this day, were being sunk into place by the bankers and politicians. Few voices were heard in protest. Political reform was the most unpopular cause that a man could have embraced. But Pickett came from fighting stock. And he was young and hopeful.

The following year he entered the arena of national politics with a savage attack on the newly

---

[4] *History of California,* p. 343.

founded Republican party's presidential candidate,
Frémont. He issued a pamphlet entitled *John C. Frémont: his Character, Achievements, and Qualifications for the Presidency; and other matters connected
therewith.*[5] According to Pickett, the candidate's
character was that of a bastard and political tool,
his achievements were treasonable, his qualifications
nil. Frémont's record in California was given in detail, including the quotation of Gillespie's "American Military Operations in California" from the
Golden Era of September 30, 1855. Pickett had much
firsthand information, gained from Gilpin, Kern,
and others who had been with Frémont. The murder by Frémont's party of the Californians, José R.
Berryessa and the De Haro twins, was instanced; and
when this was questioned by Frémont's partisans,
the accuracy of Pickett's account was championed by
Jasper O'Farrell in a letter to the *Los Angeles Star.*[6]
Frémont's illegitimate parentage and his connec-
tions with Senator Benton and with Palmer, Cook
and Company were set forth by Pickett. His claims
as pathfinder and conqueror were "debunked." It
was an effective piece of campaign literature, solidly
documented and carried off with angry indignation.

Why Kit Carson himself, the brave, dashing, generous
hearted, *genuine* "pathfinder," Kit—the man to whom

----

[5] This has apparently survived in but a single copy, that in the
California State Library. It is not cited by Nevins.

[6] September 27, 1856. Reprinted in Davis, *Seventy-five Years in
California,* p. 345.

Biog.-Collection.

JOHN C. FRÉMONT:

HIS

CHARACTER, ACHIEVEMENTS, AND QUALIFICATIONS FOR THE PRESIDENCY;

AND

OTHER MATTERS CONNECTED THEREWITH.

BY CHAS. E. PICKETT.

INTRODUCTORY.

INSTEAD of meeting the arguments and rebutting by proof the well attested statements contained in the pages of this pamphlet, doubtless the usual resort, since such arguments and statements are irrefutable, will be to assail the character and motives of the writer. The political friends (with remarkably few exceptions he has no other sort) of the Black Republican nominee, will denounce the work in general terms as a vile slander upon Fremont, and accuse the author of being prompted to his task by feelings of revenge, jealousy, malevolence, party hate and blind prejudice. In California, he is too well and widely known to call for any refutation of such charges as these, when made. And besides it is as generally known and conceded, that no man has a better recollection of past events, is more correct in his facts, dates and conclusions, and forms a truer estimate of character, where he has an opportunity of judging, than he.

Some unimportant mistakes may be detected in this hastily prepared work, though if aught of error in history, misplacement of position, or misjudgment of the designs of those mentioned herein, shall appear hereafter; correction will freely and promptly be made.

WERE all our boasted intelligence and superior facilities for acquiring correct information, the fact is patent to the world, that the mass of the people of the United States are the greatest simpletons, as well as humbugers, of any other race to be found on the globe.

Acting on this known characteristic, the Whig party, in 1848, taking advantage of our martial spirit, and ancient French love of glory, and also of a propitious time, the close of the Mexican War, when this spirit ran high, brought out for a high civil office—the Presidency of the United States—(the chief hero of that war,—the brave, honest and magnanimous old General Taylor.

It was known at the time, to every ..... reading man, that however good a soldier he might be, he had not the first qualification of a statesman. In fact, as was proved afterward, and admitted by those who elected him on the popular wave which wafted him into the Executive Seat, his favorite toast, "Old Whitey," ..... have made just as competent a .... And the good-hearted, honest old gentleman ...... told them at the start ..... was .... tician, no statesman, had never voted in his life .... this .... fact only made him the more popular.

—Collections of the California State Library

TITLE PAGE OF THE FRÉMONT PAMPHLET

Fremont is indebted so much for his meretricious fame
and Presidential capital—who cannot, or could not a
few years since, read nor write, is of far superior intellect
to this humbug nominee of the Black Republicans, and
every way the better man of the two to be made President of the United States.[7]

What Pickett feared most was that Frémont's election would precipitate strife between the North and
the South. Much as he admired James Buchanan, he
regretted that the Democrats had not nominated instead the "Little Giant of the West," Stephen A.
Douglas. He saw that the struggle between North
and South was approaching a climax. A fighting
Democratic president would augur a victory for the
South. He was confident, however, that Frémont
would be defeated. In the *Golden Era* he published
an offer to bet a thousand acres of land on the Sacramento River that the Republicans' nominee would
not be elected, or the same acreage that Buchanan
would carry California.[8]

[7] *John C. Fremont,* p. 14.
[8] October 26, 1856.

10

Orator and Epistolographer

IN 1857 Pickett prepared an address on "The Birth,
Character and Mission of Christ," to be given as
an Easter oration. It was in vain that he waited on the
ministers of San Francisco; none would permit him
use of a church auditorium in which to speak. Pickett swallowed his chagrin; and a few months later, in
Sacramento, his chance came. In the Congregational
church of that town he delivered a new, Fourth of
July oration. It was published later in the summer,
in revised and extended form, under the title, *Oration delivered in the Congregational Church, Sacramento, California, July 4, 1857*. It was the most
pretentious and polished of all his efforts up to that
time. The title page bore epigraphs by C. E. Pickett,
Jesus Christ, and Bishop Taylor.

It was a jeremiad on the state of affairs in California and the nation. Turning back for inspiration
to the pamphlets of Thomas Paine, Pickett developed with vigor his thesis that the country was fac-
ing either revolution or dictatorship.[1] The lust for

---

[1] On January 29, 1856, Pickett presided at a dinner in San Francisco in honor of Paine's anniversary. *Daily California Chronicle*,
January 30, 1856.

gold, the degenerate state of the courts, the drunken legislators, the immigrant Irish political bosses, the restless Negroes—all were viewed with alarm. Dissolution of the Union into three parts—North, South, and Pacific—was urged.

Pickett believed in the inequality of races. Efforts to absorb the Indians, the Chinese, and the Negroes were fiercely opposed by him. The natural and proper relation of mankind, he held, is that of the governing superior and servitor inferior. Development of this thought led him to issue an awful warning to

Ye women of Caucasian lineage; if not you, your daughter descendants must ere long consent to be enfolded as brides in an Ethiop's brawny embrace, and become the dams of a rising breed of tawny hybrids.[2]

Good Southerner that he was, Pickett closed his oration with an appeal to the women "to engage at once in this task of reforming our most corrupt, gross and impure society."

'Tis said that women, not men, rule the world; but in no country have such sway as in our own American land. California has formed no exception to this—few comparatively of your sex are here. But you, my chaste sisters, have thus far had but little share in the government. The fallen ones, so termed, have usurped your prerogatives, wielded the sceptre of power, and occupied a much more influential position. Queans instead of Queens, gamblers and their lemans have been crowned rulers over us all.[3]

---

[2] *Oration*, p. 21.   [3] *Ibid.*, p. 27.

The oration indicates that Pickett had been forced out of public affairs by the politicians. He was just what a man should not be for success with them: brilliant and irascible, quick to condemn and slow to forgive. His victories over the missionaries and Indian Agent White in Oregon had given him an exalted sense of his powers. In California he sought to carry on the fight against public abuses; but he underestimated the forces that were shaping the West. They were far more powerful than any one man. The bosses who had entrenched themselves, men of politics and commerce such as Broderick, Gwin, Brannan, and Coleman, wasted no time in quixotic tiltings. They understood that the westering hordes were hungry for gold and land, and by playing on the materialistic motives of greed and power they could command the situation and laugh at idealistic fools like Pickett. Not that there were many like him. In fact, Pickett was unique. No one else approached him in the length of time he spent or in the amount he wrote in the cause of reform. And instead of weakening or selling out as he aged, he gained in strength and intransigence with the years.

It was only a month after the Fourth of July oration that Pickett, from his lodgings at the Rassette House in San Francisco, issued another pamphlet, of an openly political character; its title was, *Repudiation, Supreme Judges and the Newspapers.* An election was to be held on the question of acknowledging or repudiating the admittedly unconstitutional State debt of $4,000,000. Pickett's pamphlet was a rousing and abusive call to the populace to "turn the rascals out."

Therefore my friends, or rather friends of California, do I thrice repeat—"REPUDIATE THE DEBT"—now as a stroke of great political policy—also stop paying taxes—; then after starving out the leeches, reforming affairs, killing off the credit system and growing wiser and better able, we can, if it, or a part of it, be considered a debt of honor, one binding on us, and presented in a shape where it can be indorsed and accepted in a legal mode—why we will do so, and pay it off at our convenience. Assume payment now of this fraudulent oppressive indebtedness, then farewell for years, to all hopes of reform ... Fellow citizens, this argument is sound, is true, notwithstanding the knaves and nincompoops of the California press argue the contrary.[4]

The theme of personal neglect, which was heard in the *Oration* of the previous month, appeared again in this political pamphlet.

If, after proving his devotion [Pickett wrote] to California's true interest, by years of labor in behalf of the country, at risk of life, neglect of important private affairs, and outlay of many thousands of dollars, the citizens to whom he now appeals in *their* behalf, choose not to respond to him—be the sin and suicidal ruin on their own heads. Having no family here or elsewhere to provide for, nor feel solicitous as to their fate; robbed of nearly all his once large estate; and conscious of pos-

[4] *Repudiation*, p. 6. In spite of Pickett's efforts, the debt was eventually confirmed.

sessing the worth and ability that will enable the labor of his mind to support him in some other land, where virtue and intellect are not such fatal obstacles to man's success as in California; the writer of this, with others somewhat like him, cannot be expected to live out their days among such a people, unless a better order of things be early established.[5]

The wail of the unheeded prophet was loudest in a postscript, which complained of the treatment the printed *Oration* had received at the hands of the press, and the fact that the women of California, to whom it was addressed, had remained indifferent. "The time will come, though, when, in the wail of their distress, they shall wish they had done otherwise."

Pickett was fond of complaining of the censorship exercised against him by the press; yet in all California's history probably no other man has ever had so many letters printed in the newspapers. He was a prolific correspondent, and not only to the California press; he wrote letters to the Presidents of the United States, the Governors of Virginia, to *De Bow's Review* and the *New Orleans Picayune*. No terse communications, his letters were veritable essays, many of which were collected later in pamphlet form. He should have lived in Defoe's England, when the pamphlet was at its strongest as an instrument of agitation and reform. By this time, the pamphlet was on the decline. (Today, probably the strongest senti-

[5] *Ibid.*, p. 1.

ment aroused by it is in the breasts of librarians, who despise it as troublesome to handle and to shelve.)

In 1856–57 the *San Francisco Bulletin* was Pickett's favorite medium of expression. Under a number of pseudonyms he published letters on a variety of subjects. To President-elect James Buchanan he addressed a series on "The Corruption of Politics in California," treating among other things the abuses of Federal patronage and the Committee of Vigilance (against which Pickett was arrayed); these were signed "An Old Californian" and "An Old California Pioneer."[6] Between whiles of writing this series, and under the pseudonym of "Camillus," he sandwiched in three letters on "The California Judiciary: Evils of the Present System."[7] Early in 1857 he employed the pseudonyms of "C.," "An Old Californian," and "Quartz," to keep up a steady fire on the politicians Broderick, Gwin, Weller, Latham, and Bigler.[8]

He could write about other things than politics, as he proved in a lengthy letter in the *California Chronicle* in defense of Marshall's claim to have been the first discoverer of gold.[9] But not for long could he keep from his favorite subject—reform. Its attraction for him is amusingly revealed in a series

[6] December 15, 17, 1856; January 3, 17, 1857.
[7] December 23, 26, 30, 1856.
[8] January 5, 8, 12, 14, 17, 20, 1857.
[9] January 28, 1856. Reprinted in Shuck, *The California Scrap-Book*, pp. 76–81.

of three letters to the *California Farmer*. In the first, Pickett confined himself fairly well to the matter at hand, which was the importation of sheep into California, and promised in conclusion to write further on the same subject. His next letter opened with some pastoral reminiscences, but then proceeded to flay a "maudlin sot" who had ridiculed Pickett's expression of sentiment for his sheep. Following this, he confessed to having no wife and children, but urged others to the love of a chaste woman and to "go to the country at once, and prove themselves patriots and good citizens of California, by raising as fast as circumstances will permit, all the grass, grain, grapes, chickens and children, and other animals in their power," concluding:

As for me, I have long been wedded to a bride (if I may thus personify what most persons tell me is a Utopian idea of mine, a mere chimera or hallucination of the brain)—political reform in California. By nature designed for such occupation; with ardent zeal have I for years past devoted myself to this cause. The thieves and money-changers and soul-traders must be driven from our temple of liberty. The fathers of this republic did not build it to be desecrated and have its high seats filled with such a band of plunderers as have taken possession of and polluted this western wing. Truly they have made it a den of thieves, and more unclean than Augean stables or a guano island rookery.

In another paper I shall speak more to the point on political topics—not partisan nor personal—but certain great questions appertaining to the interests of this

State, which I doubt not you, Mr. Editor, and all who have made this land their home, will fully indorse.

Sure enough, in the very next issue Pickett's letter made no mention of agriculture, but dwelt solely (and vigorously) on the necessity of limiting immigration to California. ("Our first object should be to manufacture *citizens* out of the *sojourners* now in the land.") He also called for the security of land titles.

This was his last contribution to the *California Farmer.* The editor, Colonel Warren, was apparently more interested in printing letters on farming than on politics.[10]

---

[10] Pickett's letters are found in the issues of March 20 and April 10 and 17, 1857. The MS of the first letter is in the Warren Papers in the Bancroft Library. Colonel Warren was one of Pickett's few contemporaries who preserved copies of his pamphlets; they were obtained from him by R. E. Cowan, and are now in the University of California libraries at Berkeley and Los Angeles.

II

The 'Sixties

"THE BODY politic is very sick—is moribund; and since to individual patients *in extremis,* the bold and sensible practitioner does often minister with good effect the deadliest poisons, as a dernier remedy, so I prescribe this alterative nauseous physic, to a state diseased unto death. I vote for the Lincoln electors." These words written by Pickett on the face of his ballot in the presidential election of November, 1861, spread state-wide his growing reputation for eccentric individuality. His fever for Southern rights had been steadily mounting. In 1857 he had traveled to Oregon to agitate for slavery, at the time of the debate on organization of the state government. Possibly there is reference to him in these words spoken in Congress in 1861 by Oregon's senator, Colonel Edward D. Baker,[1] in pledging the loyalty of Oregon and California to the Union: "There are a few men there who have left the South for

[1] Carey, *History of Oregon,* II: 778. Pickett's opinion of Baker is given in a letter he wrote to J. W. Nesmith from San Francisco, dated August 25, 1860, and preserved in the Oregon Historical Society collections.

the good of the South, who are perverse, violent, destructive, revolutionary, and who are opposed to social order."

In 1860 Pickett issued a pamphlet called *Gwinism in California,* in which he opposed the reëlection of Senator William M. Gwin. His other *bête noire,* Broderick, had been removed from the political scene the year before by Terry's well-aimed pistol shot. Pickett arraigned his fellow Southerner, Gwin, on two counts: first, for his stranglehold on Federal patronage in California (which, of course, excluded Pickett from any office), and second, for what Pickett termed his "spurious Southernism." This time, Pickett was to come out the winner. Gwin, by his attempt to ride three horses at once (the North, the South, and a proposed Pacific Republic), helped bring about his own downfall. Although he was to live another twenty-five years, his political career ended in this defeat. The unsavory part played by him in the Terry-Broderick duel contributed to his eclipse. He was replaced as senator by James A. McDougall. The other senatorial representative from California was Milton S. Latham, who had been elected to replace the dead Broderick.

When Lincoln was elected President, Pickett's other political point was carried. His exaltation was nearly boundless. To Senator Latham he addressed a series of letters urging him to use his influence in Washington to help swing California over to the

Southern cause.[2] To the California press he penned inflammatory letters, prophesying and calling for the disruption of the North. So violent were these letters in abuse of the press that Pickett had some difficulty in getting them printed. A glance at the captions for one, which were supplied by him, will show the state he was in.

TERRIBLE NEWS FROM THE NORTHERN STATES

Nemesis demands her own,
Acteon devoured by his hounds.

Sanguinary Progress of the Revolution—Lincoln, Seward, Greeley, Webb, Bryant, Lovejoy, Giddings, Garrison, Geritt Smith, Wendell Phillips, John W. Forney, Fred Douglas, Stephen A. Douglas, and many other Abolition leaders hung, shot, and otherwise slain by infuriate mobs of their recent partizans—Hundreds of Abolition clergymen share the same fate, and their churches destroyed—Destruction of Printing Presses—State and City Governments powerless—Chaos and a conflict of arms everywhere the order of the day—People divided into numerous factions, and all fiercely assaulting each other— A bloody war of races begun—All business suspended, starvation among the poor, and thousands of desperate persons of both sexes demanding bread or blood!— Cities sacked and fired!—Agrarian doctrines openly pro-

[2] Though violent and extreme, Pickett was a man of firm ideals and principles. This is nowhere better shown than when he reprinted his letters to Latham, with this note of explanation: "Justice to Senator Latham requires I shall state, that in replies to my letters, he strongly deprecates the disunion ideas advanced therein."—*Existing Revolution*, 2d ed., p. 3.

claimed and practiced—Cry of down with the rich Aris-
tocrats!—Great Destruction of property!—Many seizing
their moveable effects and fleeing from the country—
Millions of capital being transferred to Europe and the
South, also some to California—Appeals to the South to
march an Army among them to restore order and protect Property and Life!—It is done![8]

In Sacramento, a month before the inauguration
of Lincoln, Pickett gathered his philippic letters
into a pamphlet called *The Existing Revolution*.
This marked the high point of his career as a Confederate agitator. The necessity of comprehending
one's epoch was a favorite theme of his. From his
study of history he believed that he had arrived at
a perfect comprehension of the present and future
of the Republic. It is unnecessary to analyze in detail
Pickett's Southernism as revealed in this occasionally hysterical and entirely inflammatory pamphlet.
More interesting is its revelation of Pickett's opinion
of himself in his forty-first year. The preface opens:

In these pages will be found much food for thought.
Some will be rejected and denounced by almost all, but
this proves not such false. The utterance of all great
truths is thus ever treated; and the writer or speaker of
them, regarded as a fool, a madman or a knave. This has
always been my fate. I mind it none, except to mourn
over the ignorance and depravity of my kind, and endure that suffering such a state of society inflicts upon
me. I write not for popularity, else should tell but little

---

[8] *Alameda Gazette*, January 5, 1861. See also *San Francisco Bulletin*, November 8, 1860, and *San Francisco Call*, December 4, 1860.

truth; for all genuine philosophers tell offensive truths, and are extremely unpopular in such a corrupt age and country as this.

In this Confederate pamphlet Pickett first gave himself the name by which he is remembered—"Philosopher" Pickett. He applied it to himself in high seriousness and respect. No state can be well governed—he was fond of quoting Plato—whose philosophers are not its rulers, or whose rulers do not philosophize. He referred continually to his powers of reasoning through the aids of analogy, intuition, and induction. And to cap it all, in the San Francisco Great Register of 1867 he listed his occupation as "philosopher."

It was a bitter cup that history forced the Philosopher to drink. Within a few months his prophecy of civil conflict was realized. But it was not the North that was disrupted by revolution; it was the South that was ruined by war. The succeeding years must have been increasingly painful to Pickett as he saw his beloved South conquered by the Union armies and afterwards victimized by "reconstruction." California, as usual, ignored him, and lined up solidly with the North on the prosecution of the war; and to make it worse, it was California gold, so hated by him, which played a vital role in the war's outcome.

With unusual prudence Pickett abstained from fighting the war with his pen. He probably realized that it would have meant his being put in jail for treasonable utterances. Even former Senator Gwin was imprisoned for treason, during and after the war. It was ten years before Pickett issued another pamphlet.[4]

However, he did not go into seclusion. On April 2, 1862, Senator Hill of Santa Cruz presented in the legislature a petition by Pickett to move the capital from Sacramento several miles down the river to Sutterville. This was no lunatic idea. Sacramento was admittedly a wretched site, in constant danger of floods, which through the years played havoc with buildings and records. The deluge of January, 1862, which probably prompted Pickett's action, was among the most destructive; the entire city was flooded, and traffic proceeded in boats. In fact, Governor Stanford was rowed to his inauguration.

The reception given to Pickett's memorial was not favorable; in fact, the proceedings smacked of burlesque, as is shown in the following report given by the *Sacramento Union:*

... Mr. Hill presented a memorial from an old Californian, he said, who had been in the country since 1846–7. He had not read it, but glanced over sufficiently to see that it related to the State Capital. As the Committee on Claims had reported, he moved to place it on file with the bill on the same subject.

Mr. Nixon thought it was due to the Senate to name

---

[4] To the *Alta* of December 29, 1861, he contributed an eloquent obituary notice of William D. Fair—"one of the few in California entitled to the name of *gentleman,* in the true meaning of the word."

the author of the memorial. He was a gentleman noted for his vagaries and erratic conduct generally—Mr. Charles E. Pickett. [Laughter.]

Several Members—"Read!" "Read!"

The question was taken on reading, and lost. The memorial will come up with the bill . . .

Mr. Porter called for the reading of the memorial of Charles E. Pickett. Several members objected.

Mr. Parks said it was a memorial from the Prophet Pickett. He hoped it would be read.

Mr. Hill said out of respect for the memorialist he thought it should be read.

The President (Mr. Merritt) said the Chair was not in possession of it, and it could not be found.

Mr. Porter hoped the memorial would be found. If such documents were to be placed, God knows where, he wanted to know what became of the sacred right of petition.

The President said he did not know where it was whoever else might know . . .

Mr. Porter hoped that memorial would be read. It contained some valuable information.

Mr. Irwin moved to refer it to Mr. Porter.

Mr. Chamberlain said he understood it was from a crazy man.

The memorial was ordered read by a vote, and the Secretary went through it in about fifteen minutes. It is a prosy repetition of speeches in the Legislature this Winter, and winds up by recommending Sutterville as the site for the genuine Sacramento of the future. The fact was also stated that the memorialist owned property there which would answer for the Capitol to stand on.

. . . Resolved, That the Clerk be required to compute the cost of time to the State consumed in the reading of the Pickett Memorial, and that the same be deducted from the per diem of the Senator from Santa Cruz. [Laughter.] Ruled out . . .[5]

The petition was certainly worth reading. It showed, among other things, that Pickett was still an amateur geologist. Following are extracts from it:

Are their [the people's] representatives right in following the suicidal and foolish example of that town [Sacramento] by outlaying large sums of money for the erection of public buildings, not only in a marsh which is subject to the periodic overflow of two large rivers, but the whole site, composed as it is, of alluvion constantly endangered being swept away by the wearing and changing currents of these rivers, and from which no artificial elevation of the streets nor levees can secure it.

From the mouth of the Sacramento River to Red Bluffs, a distance of 340 miles, there are but two approaches of continuous highland from the mountains to the river, one at Knight's Landing on the western side, which, however was but of slight elevation above the recent rise, and being for some miles back composed of alluvial soil, is too, not entirely safe from the cutting actions of the river current. The other is the bluff at Sutter [Sutterville]. This remarkable point so clearly and beneficently formed by nature for the ground plans of a large emporium, is composed of cement or tertiary sandstone, and therefore, safe against the wash and wear of the rivers, even should the currents of the Sacramento and American—as at no distant day they may—infringe directly upon it. Here then is the spot to erect the Capitol buildings around which the legitimate Sacramento

[5] April 5, 1862.

soon must grow up. It is, in fact, the spot the people of the State have, through their representatives, already voted for, because here is where the original town of Sacramento was laid off, and where everybody, including the amphibious animals of the mud hole two miles above, declare at present, their whole populace should be. An appeal has gone forth from the property-holders and others of Sacramento, not to do so ungenerous an act as remove the Capital from them, under existing circumstances. This appeal should have no weight, for two considerations; first, that the Capital was not located at Sacramento for the benefit or convenience of its inhabitants, more than their ratio of population entitled them to demand; and secondly, the greater the distress and danger they are in, by reason of the ill location of their city, the more the necessity and the duty of Legislators to remove elsewhere. As one of the proprietors of the site of Sutter, I shall object to a revival of that ignominious, corrupting, and insulting buying and bidding for the location of the seat of government in our town. If fixed upon for such a purpose let commissioners select the necessary public grounds, and agree to pay a fair consideration.[6]

The rest of the 'sixties was one of the quietest periods of Pickett's life. He engaged sporadically in a political agitation. The *Bulletin* for October 12, 1867, carried the notice, "Philosopher Pickett's speech on the *Great Political Questions of the Day* was not delivered last evening, but is announced for Tuesday night next at Dashaway Hall." The speech apparently was never given.

---

[6] *Alta California*, April 3, 1862.

He had not relinquished his claim to the land on San Francisco's Rincon Hill, although he had not been in possession of it for nearly twenty years. Decisions of lower courts and land commissions had repeatedly gone against him. The Van Ness Ordinance of 1855, whereby the city of San Francisco assented that its pueblo lands should be vested in fee in the occupants; the legislature's action in 1858 in approving this ordinance; a similar act of Congress in 1864; a Circuit and a Supreme Court confirmation: these were some of the setbacks Pickett suffered.

Still he continued to struggle. In the spring of 1868, acting as his own attorney, he appealed his suit against S. C. Hastings *et al.*, the occupants of the Rincon Hill claim, to the California supreme court. After filing the action, he left for southern California on a trip in search of health.

Arriving in Los Angeles in the early summer of 1868, he found recreation in writing letters to the San Francisco newspapers on the subject uppermost in his mind, the state of land titles. When he found out later that his letters had gone unpublished, he was vexed. In January, 1869, he turned his attention to local matters, and penned a letter to the *Los Angeles Star* (recently revived as a weekly, following suspension during the Civil War) on "Pueblo Titles and Fraudulent Surveys." It was published, with this mild note by the editor: "We publish today a communication from Philosopher Pickett. If the points he makes be well founded, then the sooner the truth is known the better, so that a remedy may be provided against the evils arising from our confessedly loose and careless way of doing business heretofore. The subject is of great importance, and a little airing of it can do no harm.'"[7]

And "a little airing" it got! Pickett's point was that the auction sales made by the Los Angeles pueblo authorities of the common lands were illegal, null, and void, and that the lands were open to homesteading. His initial letter closed with a typical Pickettian challenge to the city's chief executive: "The new Mayor, in his recent message, virtually charges that nearly the whole of the Pueblo patrimony has been swindled from the rightful owners, by a ring or certain rings of unscrupulous speculators. If not himself one of these 'ringers,' and possessed with nerve enough to do his duty, he will sanction the taking of some steps in the direction suggested by me, looking to the recovery of the booty from them."

The challenge was accepted quickly enough by the other local newspaper, the *Daily News;* its editor told Pickett that he did not know what he was talking about.[8] Whereupon the Philosopher replied to him in the next issue of the *Star,*[9] and again two weeks later in a further essay on "Pueblos—What

---

[7] January 9, 1869.   [8] January 11, 1869.   [9] January 16, 1869.

Are They?'"[10] In this he termed his opponent, the *Daily News,* "the now recognized organ and defender of the Los Angeles law-defying land grabbers." The climax of the dispute was provided by Pickett in the conclusion of his last letter to the *Star,* wherein the local attorneys got a taste of his sarcasm:

You may not have space to print them nor do I care to trouble myself to hunt up the various laws and court decisions sustaining my position upon this subject. If any wish to consult practicing attorneys in the premises, I question not but several may be found in Los Angeles possessed of *knowledge* enough to give them the required information; but whether their *interests* will permit them so to do, is a something else.[11]

With this parting shot Pickett returned to San Francisco.

---

[10] January 30, 1869.   [11] February 6, 1869.

12

Into the Fray Again

TIMES had been getting worse in California since the end of the Civil War; but in the meantime the transcontinental railway was nearing completion, and people were hoping that it would end hard times and bring back the prosperity of the gold days. In 1869 the rails were joined. The expected miracle did not happen; instead, times became harder than before. The "terrible 'seventies" set in, during which the haphazard economic structure of the State went rapidly to pieces. Speculative mining ventures collapsed; banks failed; and in the wake of this general debacle many of the new industries and businesses created by the advent of the railway failed. Land monopoly, against which Pickett had been fighting for years, became so restrictive that in 1870 one five-hundredth of the population of California owned more than one-half of the available agricultural lands of the State.

If this greatest depression in all of California's history had not occurred, Pickett's later years would probably have been very different from what they were. As a political prophet and reformer he had been completely discredited by the defeat of the South. Nevertheless, the bitter 'seventies provided a fertile field for the reformer to work in. Expropriated and hungry people lent willing ears to those who preached in protest against prevailing conditions. It was not by chance that Henry George and his single-tax theory made their appearance in California at this time. Many voices joined Pickett in his cry for reform.

And Pickett himself was at his busiest. Between 1871 and 1880 he issued more pamphlets than during all the rest of his career.

But before we follow the Philosopher through the checkered course of his final years, this seems a proper time to inquire into his personal characteristics; to ask about his appearance, where and how he lived, and how he was regarded by his fellows. It would probably not surprise anyone who has followed Pickett's life thus far, and he has reached the age of fifty, to learn that the polemical pamphleteer who had blasted his way through three decades was a bitter, solitary crank. But such he was not. On the contrary, Pickett was affable, gregarious, philosophical in his quotidian habits, and liked by nearly everyone, including his political enemies. Shuck tells us that "he always carried an unfailing supply of fun, in the form of anecdotes and reminiscences, and this tended to make him companionable. Of a temperament not favorable to friendship, he yet made very few real enemies. Few men have ever been so well known over the whole coast."[1]

It was only when he took pen in hand that he became solemn, violent, and abusive. Even when the Civil War was brewing, and he was extremely agitated, he retained his ability to maintain friendly social intercourse with his fellows. This is revealed in an excerpt from his Civil War pamphlet, in which he wrote, "however lightly and in *ad captandum* style I may converse upon this topic in the streets and other public places (forced so to do to meet the wishes, comprehension, and similarly expressed contrary ideas of the shallowheads I talk to), it is of too serious and momentous import for me to jest about in print."[2]

In his "Illustrations of Life and Character" Bancroft has left us a satirical portrait of Pickett, which is worth giving in full:

San Francisco, as well as Athens, had its Diogenes. Philosopher Pickett was his name. Between Pickett and his Athenian prototype there existed certain differences incident in some measure to differences in age and country. For example, instead of rolling in hot sand, and clasping snow-clad statues, the Californian philosopher sunned himself on the piazza of his hotel, and drank iced juleps. His tub stood in the lobby of the legislature, where he practiced the profession of commanding men.

---

[1] *History of the Bench and Bar in California,* p. 367.
[2] *Existing Revolution,* p. 18.

However at heart a cynic, the surface was charmingly bland. So it always was with Californian philosophers. Of whatsoever school, the very first requisite was a free and easy demeanor. This, with always a readiness to drink at someone else's expense, and a happy faculty of impelling the hands of listeners into their pockets for the benefit of a bar-room company, were qualities in obtaining an ascendency over the mind more fruitful than flagellations, chastity, poverty, or any species of antics or asceticism.

Office-seekers were not slow to perceive that Philosopher Pickett was endowed with qualities of great value to everyone except himself. It is enough for a philosopher to be a philosopher. The moment he seeks wealth or political preferment the pedestal crumbles, and he becomes like other men, earthy.

Once a candidate for a legislative clerkship, noticing the extended acquaintance and easy influence of the philosopher, determined to approach him. The little man was courteous, and very free with his half dollars about bars and billiard tables. In due time the applicant for office broached the subject nearest his heart, and begged the philosopher's influence. Pickett turned to him in apparent surprise, as if the man's every movement for the past three days had not discovered his ambition, and straightening his figure to its full height, fixed upon him a pair of glittering gray eyes, and spake:

"Sir," said he, "I am the last man outside of Plato's republic from whom you should solicit aid. Should I advocate your claim, the members would suspect you honest; and surely you must know that an honest man stands no more chance before a California legislature than a cat in hades without claws." The language of Californian philosophers, it will be observed, is more forcible than eloquent. "If you want office," continued Pickett, "cheat at poker, brawl o'nights, murder a man or two, show your breadth at bribery—anything rather than display such weak imperfections as honor, honesty, and good character. Our legislators will none of these."[3]

This description of his eyes as being gray, and Shuck's reference to his peculiar gate and his height and weight as being a little above the average, are the only details of Pickett's physical appearance that have been recorded. No photograph of him is to be found. Pictures of other members of his Virginian clan have in common long faces, high foreheads, and prominent bony noses. Such may well have distinguished the intrepid Philosopher.

According to Shuck, Pickett had "an invisible means of support." After the loss of his property subsequent to the Gold Rush, there is no record of his having received any income apart from the $9500 refunded him by the legislature in 1852. The San Francisco directories from 1866 to 1882 give his local address, and in addition to a place of residence (generally a boarding house) he is listed as having an office with various attorneys. In the late 'sixties it was with Thornton and Williams, and in the 'seventies with John B. Harmon. It is likely that he eked out a living by doing clerical work for these lawyers. Possessed of a fine regular hand, and versed in legal phraseology and procedure, Pickett was well qualified to be useful as a scribe, and perhaps as a server

---

[3] *California inter Pocula*, pp. 367–368.

of processes and subpoenas. Certainly he was at home in any society, and fearless. For these services he was given desk space and a pittance.

In 1871, after a ten-year retirement, Pickett re-entered the fray as a pamphleteer. The occasion was a labor dispute between the miners and their employers in Amador County. When Governor Haight ordered militia from San Francisco to the mines to quell the disturbance, Pickett gave voice to outraged public opinion in *A Letter from Charles E. Pickett to Jno. A. Eagan, Secretary of the Amador Miners' League, and other matter*. After disposing of the governor ("a piebald nondescript") as a tool of "Reese, Latham, Colton and Co. and others of their ilk (as selfish and unscrupulous a set of grasping speculators and extortioners as this city, *par excellence,* of human sharks can show)," he sounded the call for a third party. Although he had remained more or less loyal to the party of his birth, he was now led to damn the Democrats along with the Republicans as "rotten and effete old parties." The new party was to have the following watchwords:

Down with the Money Power!
Down with the trafficing Politicians!
Down with the mercenary and pandering Newspapers!
Restoration of all the Public Domain, given or sold to speculators, to the common property!

After prophesying a revolutionary uprising of the people of California, he signed his pamphlet "Charles

Edward Pickett, for thirty years an unawed, uncompromising and continuous assailant of the exploiting Moneyocracy, and their co-operating congeners, the trafficing Politicians." It is apparent that Pickett's style had suffered no ossification in the ten-year lapse.

The following year he addressed a printed document to the Legislature, entitled *Protest and Memorial against Granting Appropriation to the Immigrant Aid Society*. It appears that the great landowners were encouraging foreign (chiefly Chinese) immigration in order to obtain a more than ample reservoir of population from which cheap labor could be drawn when needed. Pickett reiterated his belief that, rather than bring in new hordes, something should be done to improve the condition of the working people already in California. He protested against the idea that governments are instituted and laws enacted primarily and chiefly for the protection of property instead of for the protection of individuals. Land monopoly was thus described:

Almost the entire area of arable public land in California, as well as the major portion of the Mexican and Spanish granted ranches, having passed into the proprietorship of a few speculators, at insignificant prices—chiefly through the tortuous and unfair agencies of corrupt legislation and adjudication—it is the height of presumption for these *legal spoliators* or robbers within the pale of the law, of this vast estate and other wealth of the country, to come before the people's representatives seeking such subsidy to increase population, only to enhance the value of their possessions.[4]

In 1874 there came before the State Assembly two concurrent socialistic resolutions, introduced by Mr. Tully, of which Pickett claimed the authorship. He was refused the use of the Assembly chamber to give an address in support of the resolutions. Whereupon he printed his remarks, "with unparliamentary additions," in pamphlet form, under the title, *Address of Charles E. Pickett to the California Legislature, upon the Government Fee in the Public Domain— Inter-Communication and Land Monopolies and Correlative Topics.*

The resolutions endorsed by him were, in brief, that public lands be parceled out only in 160-acre lots to actual occupants, and all former grants to revert to the common estate; and that all highways, railways, telegraph lines, and so on, be government-owned, and the cities own all utilities. Henry George and his single tax did not have Pickett's approval; they were too radical! He had this to say about George:

Nor do I agree with that class of well-meaning but Utopian reformers who advocate all taxes being assessed upon land, and this tax to be increased in the ratio of one's holding, until it amounts to a virtual confiscation. This is violative of principle. It is employing one evil to correct another. Man is, by nature a monopolist, and

[4] *Protest and Memorial*, p. 1.

if one shall acquire property fairly and through the operations of just laws, he should be equally protected in his estate, however bulky this may grow.[5]

On the whole, this is one of the most sensible of Pickett's pamphlets. In the light of today's practices it is not very radical. He showed good sense in his stand against petty economies in the State's government. To lower the salaries of such officials as are required to conduct the government was not economy, but a bid for incompetent men to fill these offices and an encouragement to official malfeasance. Instead of lowering the governor's salary to $6000 a year, Pickett held that it should be raised to $12,000. Instead of fulminating at length against the justices of the California Supreme Court, who had recently decided against him in a land suit, he merely aimed one sentence at them, and a good one it is: "I would recommend the plan pursued by King Cambyses of Persia, who had a corrupt Chief Justice skinned alive, and the skin fastened over the judgement seat, for his successors to sit upon, and thus be always warmingly reminded of his fate, and what caused it."

This adverse decision by the Supreme Court was a bitter blow to him, for it marked the end of his hopes ever to recover his claim on Rincon Hill. True, his suit could be appealed to the United States Circuit and Supreme courts, but such procedure required money, and the impecunious Philosopher

[5] *Address*, p. 10.

was still dependent upon his "invisible means of support." At least he had gone down fighting. Two of the State's best land-title lawyers, John W. Dwinelle and John B. Harmon, had argued the case for him; and the court's decision against him, given by Associate Justice Augustus L. Rhodes, was not unanimous: Associate Justice E. W. McKinstry read a dissenting opinion.[6]

[6] *Reports of Cases Determined in the Supreme Court of the State of California, at the October Term, 1873 and January Term 1874,* pp. 269–291.

13

De-chairing a Justice

P<small>ICKETT</small>'s wrath against the Supreme Court smoldered for several months before it broke out in the most quixotic act of his life. This was occasioned by the question of the terms of office of the Supreme Court justices. In 1871 the court referred the question to Joseph P. Hoge, Samuel H. Wilson, and Samuel H. Dwinelle; the first two being at the head of the bar and the last a district judge. They unanimously held that there was no such thing as a short term so far as an election by the people was concerned; that, when the governor appointed a person to fill a vacancy, such person held until the next election; but that whenever there was an election by the people the person elected took the office for a full term.

Neither the legal profession nor the public ever accepted this view, and it was eventually repudiated in the new State constitution adopted in 1879. The original constitution said, "The justice having the shortest term to serve shall be the Chief Justice." Now if all elected justices held for full terms, it would occur now and then that there would not be any justice whose term was shortest, but there would be two justices with terms equally "short."

The opinion of the legal commission appointed to determine the question affected the terms of Justices A. C. Niles and J. B. Crockett. By all previous rule Niles's term would end on January 1, 1876. He had been elected to succeed Sanderson, who had resigned six years before at the end of his term. Crockett's term would expire on January 1, 1874. He had first been appointed in place of Shafter, who resigned December 11, 1867, leaving six years unserved. Crockett served until the next election (1869), when he was chosen by the people to serve out the remainder of Shafter's term. But both of these justices, under the opinion accepted by the court, continued on the bench until the opening of the year 1880.

When, after the opening of the year 1874, Crockett did not step off the bench, as the State constitution indicated that he should, the Philosopher unphilosophically began to gather his anger. Coming on the heels of the decision against him, it was more than he could stand. His legal friends from whom he sought an opinion all agreed that Crockett was holding his seat illegally.

Pickett's first step was to obtain the introduction of a petition in the State Assembly, "alleging irregularities by members of the Supreme Court, and ask-

ing for their impeachment." Pending the reading of
the document, Speaker M. M. Estee ruled it out of
order.[1] Pickett also managed the introduction into
that body of a resolution instructing the Judiciary
Committee to ascertain and report whether or not
Justice Crockett was the usurper of a seat on the
Supreme bench. No action was had on it.

This was the crowning indignity. Pickett evolved
a plan of action that would call the people's attention to the obvious illegality of Crockett's tenure.
When he confided in his friend, former Chief Justice John Currey, what he intended to do, the judge
said to him, "If you do that, you will land either in
jail or in a lunatic asylum!"

Pickett was not dissuaded. He had tried peaceful
and democratic means of righting a manifest wrong.
The time had come for extraordinary action.

It was on the morning of August 6, 1874, at the
opening of the Supreme Court, that Pickett acted—
and his was an act that has no parallel in the judicial
annals of California. A few minutes before eleven he
took his position at the bar among the lawyers, having previously announced his intention of making
a motion before the court. The custom of the court
was to file in, stand erect, the bar at the same time
rising to their feet in front of the bench. The bailiff
would then announce "The Supreme Court of the

---

[1] California Legislature, 20th sess., *Assembly Journal,* Vol. 69,
1873–74, p. 923.

State of California," and the members of the bar would bow respectfully. The court would then return the salute, and all would be seated.

On this particular morning Chief Justice Wallace entered first, closely followed by Justices Crockett, Niles, and McKinstry. While they were in the act of arranging themselves, previous to bowing and being seated, and just at the moment that the bailiff made his announcement, Philosopher Pickett suddenly advanced from his place among the lawyers and, stepping quickly in front of Crockett, deliberately took the seat assigned to that justice.

For a moment the courtroom was transfixed, while the intruder defiantly gripped the arms of his massive chair. Then Chief Justice Wallace called out, "Where is the bailiff of this court? Who is this man that intrudes himself?" The bailiff failing to appear, Wallace laid his hand on Pickett, as though to give him an earnest hint to vacate the seat. Whereupon Pickett, not budging an inch, raised his voice and declared, "Crockett is a bogus justice! I have as much right to this seat as he!" Then he seized the Chief Justice and showed determination to fight for his place.

By this time the court was in the wildest confusion. After a stiff melee the doughty Philosopher was finally overpowered by the clerk and the crier. Wallace then ordered him to be put into the street, and at the same time said: "This man is guilty of contempt of court. We fine him $500 and order him to prison for five days and until the fine is paid."

As he was being ejected from the chamber, Pickett got an arm free, and shaking his fist at the bench, cried, "I defy you!" Wallace was quick to respond. "We fine you $500 more," he intoned. And the oaken doors slammed on the Philosopher.

To jail Pickett went. His sentence was fixed at one day for every two dollars of the fine due from him, or five hundred days, plus the original sentence of five days, making a total of five hundred and five days to be served. (Later, Pickett said he had heard from Crockett's son that the severe penalty was not so much for what Crockett senior termed Pickett's mad freak as that, he having so frequently wrongly and roughly assailed the court in the newspapers, the justice had determined, when the opportunity arose, to make him smart for it.[2] He was unable to raise the money. The San Francisco Directory for 1875 gave his address as "Branch County Jail, S.W. Corner Francisco and Stockton."

He was not long in winning over his jailers. He gained as private quarters a little sentry room on the roof of the jail, which for long after was known as the "Philosopher's fort." He was also allowed the privilege of promenading along the corridors and sitting in the office.

There was much popular sympathy for him. The

[2] *Anti-Plundercrat Pamphlet*, pp. 21–22.

hard times of the mid-'seventies had made people rebellious against authority. Recognizing this growing restiveness, several prominent jurors interceded for him, but in vain. Even the *Alta California*, the newspaper which Pickett had vilified over all others, took the Philosopher's side. In its issue of December 10, 1874, it printed a petition for his release, which was being circulated, and devoted its leading editorial to the subject:

We believe that nine-tenths of the voters of California would take pleasure in signing this petition if it were offered to them, and would even go out of their way to get the privilege of signing. Not a newspaper in the State has commended the sentence; many have condemned its severity . . . His offence was one of mistaken judgement, not malice. Many hold Crockett to have no right to his seat. We give the Court fair notice that if they persist in holding Charles E. Pickett a prisoner for the full term of 500 days, they will accumulate against them a popular prejudice that will not expire so long as they may live.

It was not until the following April, after he had been imprisoned eight months, that the petition came before the Supreme Court. A motion for his release accompanied it, signed by James A. Johnson, a veteran Democratic politician who subsequently was elected lieutenant governor. Johnson's motion declared that Pickett had intended no contempt, but had wanted only to bring before the public the facts regarding the court. Unfortunately his plans had miscarried. As for the second contempt, Pickett had hurled his words of defiance not at the chief justice, but at someone in the audience who was ridiculing him.

This amount of humble pie proved ample for the court. The remaining $500 fine was remitted. The *Alta* for April 24th carried the headline, PHILOSO-PHER PICKETT RELEASED. Wearing a martyr's robe the Philosopher came forth into the world again.

No more broken by this experience than he had been by the Civil War, he brought suit against the Supreme Court justices to recover damages in the sum of $100,000 for false imprisonment! Thereupon ensued six years of legal dispute. It was not until an entirely new group of justices occupied the bench that the court was held competent to render a decision on Pickett's appeal. In January, 1881, with Pickett appearing as counsel in his own behalf, the court was of one mind in giving him the *coup de grâce*. They wrote: "We are not aware of any principle upon which this action can be maintained. There is no question but that the Supreme Court of this State had jurisdiction to adjudge as to contempts, and to punish therefor."[8]

---

[8] *Reports of Cases ... November Session of 1880, and January and April Sessions of 1881.*

14

Philosopher versus King

AFTER his release from jail, Pickett took up the
battle on a new front. By 1876 the Central Pacific Railroad monopoly was firmly fastened on California. The need for a transcontinental railway had
always been a favorite theme of Pickett's, even as
far back as 1843 and the days of the Oregon Lyceum
discussions. When the road was finally completed
in 1869, he could not keep from taking an almost
proprietary interest in it. On the basis of his early
prophecies he felt himself entitled at least to a pass
on the C. P. R. R. Much to his vexation the company
spurned him.

In January, 1876, he issued a pamphlet against the
president of the railroad, Leland Stanford, former
governor of California and one of the "Big Four"
bosses of the State. This is the only one of his writings which Pickett issued anonymously. (His ano-
nymity however was thinly veiled, and in a later
work he referred to the anti-Stanford pamphlet as
having been written by him.[1]) He called it *The Cali-*

---

[1] *Pickett's Pamphlet on the Railway* . . . , p. 11.

fornia King: His Conquests, Crimes, Confederates, Counsellors, Courtiers and Vassals; Stanford's Post-Prandial New Year's Day Soliloquy. It is a satirical production. In a preface "The Editor" wrote:

Rebelliously seeking to learn the inside history or secret machinations of the all-powerful Occidental Railway monarch—Leland Stanford—that we might publish the same; and believing in the old Latin apothegm, "In Vino Veritas"; and knowing His Majesty's habit of imbibing freely at dinner; and then unreticently "thinking aloud" in his unreveries thereafter, we dispatched, on the evening of the 1st inst., our attending Mercury, who has the faculty of passing through keyholes, and rendering himself invisible at pleasure, to the smoking apartment in the palace of the great railway potentate, to report what he could see and hear. He brings us the following.

The Philosopher then proceeded to place his exposé of Stanford in the latter's own mouth. Pickett quickly gave himself away by having his Soliloquer score the chief justice of the Supreme Court "for his illegal and tyrannical treatment of 'Philosopher' Pickett because of the latter's peculiar essayment to arraign the court for such high-handed usurpation." The heart of the pamphlet is contained in the following paragraph—a catalogue of charges the justification of which has been borne out by history:

STANFORD: And I, too, ought to be despised and warred against by every man who has the good of his country at heart, and is possessed of the smallest ingredient of honesty and sense. True, I am developing the material re-

sources of the country, and have done much to facilitate
travel and the interchange of commodities; yet, at the
same time, in common with others like me, unjustly ag-
gregated the wealth of the country, sapped the moral
foundation of the Government, and spread pollution
through every ramification of society. By artfully ap-
pealing to their cupidity and constantly tempting them,
we have rendered unfaithful to their trusts and venally
implicated with us numerous public servants, from and
including the President of the Republic, down to the
lowest state and municipal official. Likewise, we have,
directly and indirectly, through the liberal dispensa-
tion of fees and largesses, induced those two influential
classes—the lawyers and the newspaper proprietors—to
sophistically pervert the laws, delude and mislead the
people, debauch public sentiment, and erect and render
paramount our *imperium in imperio*.[2]

An anecdote has been preserved which gives another view of the Pickett-Stanford relationship. It
probably antedates the publication of *The California King*. In composing his reminiscences years later,
one George E. Barnes wrote:

Pickett was disposed to cultivate the railroad magnates,
but Stanford would not have it, and sent him to the
right-about—"exiled him from his presence," as the Philosopher termed it.... Pickett used to hang about the
state capitol when the legislature was in session, picking
up odds and ends of information as to what was gonig
on, for the benefit of whom they might concern. It was
the time the late Governor Stanford was doing what he
pleased with our solons at Sacramento. One day the

[2] *California King*, p. 13.

Governor happened to leave the capitol in company
with two or three state senators. The "banished Philosopher," who was on hand, managed to catch Stanford's
eye. Then he struck an attitude, and declaimed with
a dramatic air and in a strident voice

> More true joy Marcellus, exiled, feels,
> Than Caesar with the Senate at his heels.

The Governor laughed and the senators joined with
him. The story goes that Stanford sent for Pickett
shortly afterward, and had a chat, and that when the
Philosopher left the gubernatorial presence, he did not
go empty-handed.[3]

Four months later *The California King* was followed by *Pickett's Pamphlet on the Railway, Chinese,
and Presidential Questions.* The author proposed
two means for breaking the Central Pacific monopoly: first, regulation of railway by the State legislature—that is, by a railroad commission,—and the
other, the establishment of a competing southern
line. To this latter end he had addressed a series of
letters to Jefferson Davis in Tennessee. These communications, together with Davis' polite reply, were
included in the pamphlet.[4]

As to the Chinese, Pickett's attitude was sensible.
He did not share the violent prejudice against the
Orientals which was rampant in California, holding

---

[3] "Pickings from the Past," *San Francisco Bulletin,* October 3,
1896.

[4] Pickett was still in communication with his brother, with whom
he had made his home when a youth; the Davis letters were sent in
care of William S. Pickett.

them, instead, to be "intelligent, industrious, economical, ingenious, freemen and freedom-loving." However, he recognized the problem of their presence as a real one. He had always opposed the encouragement of mass immigration into the State, and now he saw his alarms justified. "Indeed," he wrote, "ever since the foundation of our government, we have been spreading our nets all over the globe to catch and haul in all sorts of human species without regard to race or quality. We have at length 'caught a Tartar.' The question is, what shall we do with the troublesome animal?"

Times kept getting worse. In 1875 there had been a mining-stock panic, when within three weeks the values of securities listed on the San Francisco Stock Exchange declined sixty million dollars. It was then that the greatest bank failure in the State's history occurred: the Bank of California was forced to close as a result of an unbridled speculation in mining ventures engaged in with the bank's funds by the bank's president, William C. Ralston. The day after the bank closed, Ralston drowned himself in the Bay.

Ever since the completion of the railway had brought the release of thousands of Chinese coolies, the unemployed whites had become increasingly dissatisfied with the presence of the Orientals. In January, 1877, there was a severe business crisis, brought on by the announcement that the Consolidated Virginia Mines would not pay the customary million-dollar dividend. All that was needed to bring the great popular unrest to a head was a leader. In spite of the rather exaggerated opinion he had of his own talents, Pickett was obviously not the man. He was too much an intellectual and a philosopher, lacking in brute driving force. It took a drayman with a ready, coarse wit and an Irish brogue to play the role. Dennis Kearney, the immigrant of 1868 who had just been naturalized an American citizen, commenced his meteoric career as a mob leader, and rapidly took over leadership of the newly formed Workingmen's Party.

Throughout the summer and autumn of 1877, mass meetings were held on the empty sand lots of San Francisco. Kearney was violent, inflammatory, vituperative, grossly abusive and insulting. Hang the capitalists, he cried, and burn their dwellings! The mob lifted its eyes to the rococo mansions on Nob Hill. "The Chinese Must Go!" became the cry of the oppressed in their need of a scapegoat. Hoodlum gangs roamed the streets. It was rumored that plans were afoot to burn the docks of the Pacific Mail Steamship Company and then pillage Chinatown.

It was a critical situation. Led by a merchant, William T. Coleman, the Vigilance Committee reappeared, armed with hickory pickhandles. Kearney and other ringleaders were arrested and held until passions cooled. Pickett, who had been trying his skill as a sand-lot orator, was twice arrested and incarcerated, but was never brought to trial.[5]

Pickett was not a disciple of Kearney. Years before the Irish drayman had arrived in California, the Philosopher had been calling for political and economic reform. He did not share the facile belief of the moneyed class that Kearneyism was the cause of the social unrest that was troubling the State. Rather, Dennis Kearney and the sand-lot agitation—and, of course, Pickett himself—were the effects of causes which had been operating unchecked ever since the Gold Rush. It was part of Pickett's pride in himself as a philosopher that, unlike most of his contemporaries, he was able to distinguish between causes and effects. Such was the hallmark of a true philosopher.

[5] Hittell, *History of California*, IV: 605–609.

15

Pedagogy and Paris

THE YEAR 1877 was full of excitement for Pickett. On and off the sand lots, in and out of jail, he was feverishly active. When he learned that a Granger convention was to be held in San Francisco in April, to investigate the defects in the current educational system and suggest remedies, he prepared an address for the occasion. Needless to say, it was not delivered; for it was a thoroughly radical critique of the times. Not discouraged by this rebuff, he issued it in pamphlet form under the comprehensive title, *American Education Analyzed; or, a Synoptical Disquisition on the Quality, Culture, Development, Rank and Government of Man; With an Addendum describing the Order of Men to Select for Office.* It proved to be a mixture of Pickett's ideas and prejudices. That he went unpreferred as an office holder by voters and politicians alike, and that he had been several times jailed for exercising his constitutional right of free speech and assembly, galled him. With his usual frankness he sketched the popular attitude toward himself.

In degenerate eras, especially in a Republic, the virtuous patriot must rely alone upon an approving con-
science for his reward in serving society, since the cross,
the gallows, hemlock or other poison, mob violence, os-
tracism, starvation, trumped-up charges for enjailment
or confinement in lunatic asylums, or artfully popular-
ized opinion as to their harmless, unsound mentality,
else being disaffected, revolutionary, Ishmaelitish, or
visionary characters, in order to bring ridicule upon or
prejudice to bear in annulling their efforts at reform,
are, usually, meted to those rare Christly and Socratic
individuals who essay to do good to their countrymen.[1]

Pickett's critique of education was not unreason-
able. He found more trade education to be desirable,
inasmuch as the prevailing system tended to turn
out all captains and no privates, all foremen and no
workmen. Military training was recommended for
all young men. The mentally defective and mal-
formed should, as in Sparta, he drowned at birth.
The chief object of education was to enable the intellect better to comprehend, enunciate, and practice Truth. Temperance was to be practiced in all
things.

He commented at length upon the young University of California. When the institution was founded
in 1868, Pickett executed a will in which he be-
queathed a proportion of his Rincon Hill claim (if
and when awarded to him by the courts) to endow
a Professorship of Ethnology and Anthropology.

---

[1] *American Education*, p. 28.

Nine years later, in this pamphlet, he presented himself as a candidate to fill the chair, if it should ever be created. "With the sound teachings disseminated from such curriculum would necessarily be connected certain fundamental ideas upon Governmental organisms and political economy—the loftiest of all the sciences." But of course!

The president of the University, John LeConte, won Pickett's praise as the embodiment of the science of Aristotle and the ideals of Plato. And of the institution itself he wrote:

For the good of the State it is to be hoped that some of our wealthy citizens will assist in better endowing this catholic seminary of High Learning. Having sapped, as the most of them have, through their tortuous begettings, the virtuous supports and political safeguards of society, let them use some of that wealth in maintaining this conserving educational appliance. Such bestowment will operate as a sort of salve to their guilty consciences, will be a partial reparation of their committed wrongs; and their contemporaries, as well as posterity, will be disposed to rub out some of the black marks against them and insert these white ones.

Pickett lamented the absence in California of a landed gentry similar to that of England, France, and the South. Here all the country's money was in the hands of the urban Dollercrats, the *nouveaux riches* of Nob Hill who spent all on their city mansions and trips abroad. He preached a return to the soil, an agrarian revolution, to regain for the small farmers the lands of California which had passed en bloc into the hands of the urban speculators and monopolists.

Farmers [he said], inform your sons that these common estate lands are theirs, by right of inheritance and political compact, and should revert to and be taken possession of by them—if not by regular procedure, then by irregular. Keep your children and yourselves from wishing or making a home in villages, towns or cities. This undue concentering, or over-herding, is the great bane of society. My heart-yearnings [he went on to say] have ever been for rural scenes and occupations, away from the annoyances, impurities and artificialities of cities, where I can better *rapport* my soul with Nature, feast my senses upon her adornments and motherly ministrations, and invigorate my health. But here I am directed to remain the better to accomplish the great mission of my life. I never visit the country except with delight, and never leave it except with regret.

The pamphlet is also interesting for its lively remarks on certain individuals distasteful to the author. First among these was Chief Justice Wallace, the man who had jailed Pickett three years before. On him the Philosopher wreaked an anthropological revenge:

The American physique is growing less indicative of a high type of the homo. There is a less manly bearing and carriage, and the head has a less dignified, erect and symmetrical poise upon the body. It is being projected more and more pronely forward, whilst a prognathous growth of the underjaw is painfully apparent—all going to prove a retrocession towards the inferior or brute animal similitude. In fact, we are rapidly lapsing to a sort of civilized barbarism. One of the conspicuously marked specimens of this exterior and visible revealment of a sinful and beastly nature can be seen in the gross and guilty-speaking countenance and unsymmetrical and vulgar humped-up head and body coupling of the *de facto* Chief Justice of the Supreme Court of California—William T. Wallace.[2]

The old Roman apothegm *De mortuis nil nisi bonum* Pickett branded as humbug, especially in the case of the late W. C. Ralston, the plunderer of the Bank of California. Bancroft was ridiculed for his proposed *Contemporary Biography of California's Representative Men.* "Herein," said the Philosopher, "will be a grand collection of our shoddy Aristocracy. They will write the outlines of their own biographies which then will be fixed up in style by the facile penmen in Bancroft's employ. But what a vast deal in the career of numbers of these gentry will be suppressed; especially as to the various villainous methods through which the most of them acquired their fortunes. The one virtue in their lives will be transmitted to after times, but not the linked thousand crimes."[3] He threatened to write a supplement after it was published, which would serve as a key to the true characters of the men included.

The time's great agnostic, Robert G. Ingersoll, came in for a spirited denunciation as a "material-

[2] P. 16.   [3] P. 12.

istic, blathering demagogue ... a pretender ... one who has the *semblance* only of true knowledge; and hence his immense popularity among the inane multitude who applaud his fustian rhetoric and shallow reasoning."[4]

A glimpse is afforded us of Pickett's own religious evolution, in a paragraph reminiscent of the young atheist of thirty years earlier, who, together with Lieutenant Kern and other cronies, had shocked their fellow God-fearing pioneers:

> For years I labored with zeal as a sort of deistical icono-clast to destroy the waning faith of myself and others in the reality of visions, fables, ghosts and miracles, as well as express doubts of a spiritual existence beyond the grave. But I now question whether I have rendered myself the happier thereby. I think it better to relate to children or let them peruse, and believe truthful, these thaumaturgic and fairy stories, and indoctrinate them with some sort of religious belief.[5]

After this pedagogical pamphlet, and at the height of his sand-lot activities of the autumn of 1877, Pickett launched another quixotic (or shall we say, Pickettian?) project for improving his position in society. It marked the peak of his resentment at the treatment he was receiving from the courts, the newspapers, the police, and the politicians. Throughout October and November there appeared in the *San Francisco Examiner* a series of letters by him which

---

[4] P. 30.   [5] Pp. 28–29.

traced his activities all the way back to his coming to the Coast in 1843. These letters were penned with an ulterior purpose. He had conceived a plan which would enable the State to make up to him for all the abuse he had suffered at the hands of the monopolists and their venal agents.

And what a plan it was! The question had arisen, how California was to participate in the exposition to be held at Paris in 1878. The Immigration Union held that it was a prime opportunity to solicit French agricultural labor to emigrate to California. In opposing this idea, Pickett proposed sending to Paris a commission whose main purpose would be, not to advertise California, but to study and report on the superiorities of France. "I regard the Commissioner specimens," he wrote, "as the most important contribution to send. If the state shall select Commissioners, let them be men of brains and patriotism—gentlemen of culture and refinement, possessing general information, and who will do honor to us all; and not some brawling politicians or selfish money-seekers, who will be governed alone by what may conduce to their special interests and private ends."[6]

As one of the commissioners, whom should Pickett choose but—himself! He had done the State some service and they knew it, said he, echoing Othello; and although he freely admitted having erred in the course of his life, he proudly claimed an unsullied

[6] *San Francisco Examiner*, October 26, 1877.

escutcheon. Nor had he ever been sued for libel by those whom he had attacked! Gathering these newspaper reminiscences together into a pamphlet, he prefaced them with a plea for Governor Irwin's support. This was titled, *The Paris Exposition and Other Expositions: Some Leaves from the Life of a Pacific Slope Pioneer of 1842.*[7]

Then, with his pockets filled with copies of the pamphlet, the Philosopher went to Sacramento, where the legislature was in session. In the old, familiar halls the good-natured anecdotist set to lobbying. Such was his success that on January 16, 1878, Assembly Bill No. 224 was introduced by Mr. Backus. This was "An Act to provide for a Proper Display of the Industries and Resources of California at the French Exposition of 1878, and Reports upon the Same." Its gist was as follows:

1. Appointment of three Commissioners to arrange the exhibit, serve as expositors, and prepare a pamphlet in English, French and German on California's attractions.

2. Commissioners to subscribe to an oath that they have no pecuniary interest in any article exhibited, and do not act as an agent for any exhibitor.

3. Each Commissioner to receive $2500 for services and personal expenses.

4. A sum of $30,000 to be provided for general expenses.[8]

---

[7] He did not actually arrive on the Coast until 1843.

[8] *California Assembly Bills*, Vol. 2, 1877–78. See also *Alta California*, February 19, 1878.

Seated in the gallery, the Philosopher appeared quite sanguine while his bill was being read. Alas, his hopes were quickly ruined. The Assembly turned the occasion into a travesty session at his expense. The bill was immediately covered over with preposterous amendments. Among them was one inserting the names of Emperor Norton and the Gutter Snipe, two well-known street "characters" of San Francisco, as Pickett's fellow commissioners.

That was too much for even the tough-skinned Philosopher to endure. He returned to San Francisco, declaring that his friends had gone back on him. All was lost but honor, he admitted, and he abandoned his ambition to represent California at the Paris Exposition. Not the least of his disappointment was the realization that he would now probably never be able to revisit his surviving kinfolk in Virginia and Tennessee, from whom he had been separated for nearly forty years. But, unlike Othello, he did not stab himself. If one were defeated on one front, he moved to another sector and carried on the fight anew. Thus did Pickett.

16

The Anti-Plundercrat

THE "terrible 'seventies" were nearing an end. By 1878 the patience of the people was exhausted. They demanded a new State constitution which would embody the reforms agitated by the Kearneyites, Pickett, and others. Until this time California had been governed under the original constitution adopted in 1849. The convention to frame the new document met in September. Its political make-up was exceedingly motley. Among the 152 members there were 10 Democrats, 11 Republicans, 2 Independents, 78 Non-Partisans, and 51 Workingmen (Kearneyites). The railroad and corporation interests denounced the assemblage as bitterly as they had been raked by the sand-lotters. It is true that many of the resolutions introduced in the convention were impractical, confiscatory, or plainly a violation of the Federal constitution; the people's ire was running high. The document, as finally drafted, although less radical, was nevertheless repugnant to the conservatives of that time. The sessions lasted until March, 1879, when the vote was 120 to 15 for adoption. In

May the constitution was submitted to the people, and received a majority of 10,280 votes out of a total of 145,000 cast.

As viewed today, the constitutional reforms were extremely moderate. Land assessment was made more equitable; sale of water for irrigation purposes was placed under official regulation; lobbying was declared a felony; special legislation was prohibited; the railroad monopoly, which was popularly regarded as the State's greatest evil, was theoretically broken. Pickett saw his long-agitated State Board of Railroad Commissioners become a reality.

There was a period of popular rejoicing; but the battle for reform was only half won, for if the entrenched interests continued to control the legislature and the courts, the corrective and regulatory measures provided by the new constitution could in large part be nullified by lax enforcement and discriminatory decisions. Pickett saw this clearly.

Since the exposition fiasco he had published nothing. "I did, until recently, grieve much over such suicidal conduct of my countrymen, but a calm philosophic acceptance of the situation is the existing condition of my mind."[1]

But the urgent necessity for the people to clinch the constitutional reforms by electing a reform legislature prompted him to indite another pamphlet, warning of the dangers ahead. He called it *Philosopher Pickett's Anti-Plundercrat Pamphlet,* and dedi-

---

[1] *Land-Gambling,* p. 13.

cated it to "The Partially Disenthralled People of California." It was the longest pamphlet (74 pages) that he had ever published, and it served as a summary of all that he had been campaigning for

Philosopher Pickett's
ANTI-PLUNDERCRAT
Pamphlet.

A REMARKABLE PRODUCTION.
It should be read by every American.

—*Author's collection*

BROADSIDE ADVERTISING THE ANTI-PLUNDERCRAT PAMPHLET

throughout the 'seventies. Unlike nearly all his previous writings, which had been given away, this one was priced at twenty-five cents a copy. A printed broadside was issued to advertise it, an access of commercialism for which the Philosopher apologized:

This pamphlet is necessarily placed on sale, the expenses attending the delivery of the discourse[2] and its publica-

[2] "A Discourse on Law, Judges, Lawyers, *et al.;* the People versus the Plundercrats; Impending Fall of the Bourgeoisie Power; Kearneyism Analysed," delivered by Pickett in Metropolitan Temple, San Francisco, April 28, 1879. This address constituted 45 pages of the pamphlet.

tion having run me in debt some hundreds of dollars. I have given away nearly all my writings; have expended thousands of dollars in printing newspapers, pamphlets and circulars, additional to the vast amount of gratis contributions to many journals. After losing through lavish expending, and inattention to private affairs to devote myself to public ones, a once ample fortune, honorably acquired, and being swindled out of another by the plundercrats, through the instrumentality of their venal agents, the judiciary, the same spirit which prompted Marat to pawn the sheets from his bed, to pay for continuing the publication of his paper, impelled me, on more than one occasion, to pawn a portion of my scanty wardrobe to raise the money to print my free distributed pamphlets, advocating the same ideas, principles and purposes enunciated in this.

The pamphlet has been rendered more voluminous than it otherwise would, for the reason that there is not a paper in San Francisco, nor, perhaps, in all California, in the columns of which can be published an able and impartial article on public affairs, especially if emanating from my pen; hence, such matter must appear through pamphlet medium or not at all. . . . These cowardly, corrupt and defamatory newspapers have only had language of detraction, or gibberish ridicule to employ towards me. Their years of slanderous outgivings regarding me have never troubled me except to grieve that such has so greatly forestalled my influence by preventing my countrymen more heeding the many wisdom lessons I have always taught them. Instead of permitting the logic of their intellects to judge the merits of my productions, they accepted the *ipse dixit* of these mercenary sheets, that such being the emanations of an impracticable eccentric or semi-insane person, no regard should be paid them.[8]

Of course Pickett had had no more invective heaped on him than he had served out to others. San Francisco, home of Ambrose Bierce, was never noted for polite journalists. In the frequent exchanges of epithets Pickett was not hampered by an inadequate vocabulary. The charges of insanity were mostly subsequent to his freakish attempt to de-chair Justice Crockett, although as far back as Yerba Buena days he had sometimes been called "Crazy Pickett." He was never actually insane. He was hair-triggered, rash, and erratic, but not mad. He was an idealist abnormally susceptible to wrongdoing in public life. His misfortune was to have settled in a land which, within a generation, had been hustled out of its pastoral ease and excited to economic frenzy. In this overturn, in which also his personal fortunes were repeatedly reversed, Pickett was unable to keep his balance. His indignant protests at the corruption he saw flourishing on every side were bound to be ridiculed by those who were in any way dependent upon the corrupters for their existence. And anyone as relentlessly persistent in criticism as Pickett was bound to be termed a nuisance, if not a menace. Shuck supplies a pertinent anecdote:

We were in the sanctum of the *San Francisco Examiner* in 1870, sitting close to Colonel B. F. Washington, the

[8] Pp. 9–10.

editor-in-chief, and George P. Johnston, the exchange editor and part owner, when Pickett entered, holding one of his long manuscripts in his hand. Laying his paper on the editor's table, Pickett said, "I haven't put any heading on this, Washington; please read it and give it a proper caption." Johnston, always instantaneous, said, "Washington, call it *The Ravings of a Maniac*." Pickett went right out, saying nothing, but showing he was hurt.[4]

Pickett closed the decade with a return to personal polemics. A public controversy had arisen over the workings of the Consolidated Virginia Mining Company—one of the so-called Nevada bonanza firms, owned by the silver barons, Flood, Mackay, and Fair. The company was being sued for $35,000,000 by a group of its stockholders. In fighting back, the company attacked the reputation of one Squire P. Dewey, a rich San Francisco land speculator. Dewey countered with a pamphlet called *The Bonanza Mines of Nevada; Gross Frauds in the Management Exposed; Reply of S. P. Dewey to the Misrepresentations of the Bonanza Firm in their Libelous Publication of May 25, 1878*.

This served as an occasion for Pickett to pitch into the fray. In an attack on Dewey he vented the accumulated anger engendered by the loss of his suit for the Rincon Hill property. He published a pamphlet entitled *Land-Gambling versus Mining-Gambling; An Open Letter to Squire P. Dewey, Relative to his*

---

[4] *Op. cit.*, pp. 367–378.

Participation in the Land-Gambling of San Francisco in Early Days. From One Who Knows. It was not, as the title would indicate, an anonymous publication; Pickett signed his name in full to both preface and text. It is a sardonic work. He saw the squabble between Dewey and the Bonanzaites as one of "Tiger Clawing Tiger—Shark Devouring Shark," and went on to say:

For several years the voracious mining sharks have fraternally fattened on the numerous gudgeons that they conjointly enticed into their ravenous mouths and maws. But gudgeons growing scarce and lean of late, these mining stock sharks, like the "green cloth" bankers, when similarly situated, have commenced to devour each other; and when it comes to "shark eat shark," then look out for a terrific lashing, foaming and bloodying of the waters.[5]

Dewey's response to this attack on him was to spread the report that the Bonanza people had employed Pickett to pen the pamphlet. This was too much for the Philosopher. In February, 1880, he brought out an enlarged edition in which he denied Dewey's charge in an amusing figure:

Finding the Bonanza Barons and Dewey at war and fiercely bombarding each other from behind their respective ramparts, and having a grievance against the latter, I collected my own ammunition as well as taking some from the arsenals of the two belligerents, went to the rear of Dewey's fortifications, erected my battery and

[5] P. 23.

poured a heavy fire of hot shot into it. I shall continue to cannonade such enemy and all who have given or may give aid and comfort to them.[6]

To this enlarged edition a chapter called "Field-iana" was added. This was an attack on United States Supreme Court Justice Stephen J. Field. Since the Gold Rush, Field had been one of the leading judicial figures in California, and had gone to Washington from the chief justiceship of the State Supreme Court. It was he who, as a Circuit Court judge, had rendered, in 1860, the Pueblo Case decision, which eventually blasted Pickett's hope in his claim. Pickett recounted the story of the notorious "Torpedo Plot" of 1866, with its tale that Field had caused a bomb to be sent to himself in order to cast blame on those adversely affected by his Pueblo Case decision. "Field's own confession of this affair could be pumped out of him when in his cups, as he is then foolishly unreticent; so much so that at dinner parties and other drinking bouts where he frequently gets maudlin drunk, (he has been an occasional spreer since he came to California), he has to be taken away, sometimes locked in a room till he sobers off, by his friends or parties interested in some of his rascalities, lest he divulge something damaging to them, or too much disgraces himself."[7]

---

[6] Pp. 2–3.   [7] *Ibid.*, p. 20.

17

The End of the Trail

NEARLY forty years had passed since Pickett had arrived on the Pacific Coast. He was now sixty years old. Cheered by the adoption of the new constitution, though well aware of how little good it would accomplish without honest men to interpret and administer it, Pickett cast his eye back over the path he had traveled through four historic decades. Since *The Paris Exposition* his writings had been increasingly larded with personal reminiscences. In the autumn of 1880 he issued what was to prove his last pamphlet; he called it *Address to the Veterans of the Mexican War, Embodying a Historical Contrast of the Two Great Political Parties of the United States, on Vital Issues; With Personal Reminiscences and other Pertinent Episodes.* It was prepared primarily as a Democratic campaign document, but he was unable to get the State committee even to examine the manuscript, much less to provide him with funds to print it. Instead, he was "offensively rebuffed." Nor would the Veterans' Association sponsor it. The 11th of September was the anniversary of the fall of Mexico City, but the Address was not delivered. The speaker at the San Francisco celebration was General William T. Sherman. So once again Pickett published a pamphlet at his own expense. Who knows from whence the money came? From Room One, at 640 Clay Street, the author launched his last opus, to be sold at twenty-five cents a copy. In order to lay as many foes as possible, he appended to the Address three political chapters: "The California Democratic State Club Pilloried," "A New Plundercrat Organ Disguised in the Garb of Democracy," and "To the Greenback-Labor Voters."

The Philosopher was honest about the part he had played in the Mexican War as a member of the Yerba Buena Volunteers. "The Company was not marched further than Santa Clara [Pickett, as we have noted, had remained behind, to tend William Heath Davis' store!] and had but one engagement with the Hispano-California enemy, which, fortunately, proved bloodless; strategy, and a tender of the olive branch, securing us a victory. The hardest service rendered was in standing guard, during the cold and rainy nights of that dreary Winter, in the outskirts of the little village of Yerba Buena, and scouting in vicinity—since, changing its name and somewhat grown."[1] Pickett also related an episode regarding the hoisting of the American flag in Monterey in 1846 as told him by his friends, Daingerfield Fauntle-

---

[1] P. 2.

roy, purser of the *Savannah,* and Rodman M. Price, purser of the *Cyane.*[2]

The chapter headings give an idea of the pamphlet's scope; for example: "Campaign of 1844," "A Diplomatic Reminiscence (Oregon)," "Webster vs. Calhoun," "War with Mexico," "Fremont Explorations," "Gadsden Purchase," "My Railway Routes Reconnaissances," "My Early Texan Relations," "New England Nullifiers and Secessionists," "The Sectional War," "General Sherman," "Acquisition of Hawaii," "Monopolies," "Booth and Confreres," "Military Presidents," "Caesarism."

In an Appendix he pays his respects to San Francisco newspapers. The "New Plundercrat Organ Disguised in the Garb of Democracy" was none other than the *Examiner* ("all genuine Democrats should let this Pluto-Syndicate organ severely alone"). A good Democratic paper was *The Daily Globe,* and also the old pioneer weekly, *The Golden Era;* and two recommended Greenback-Labor organs were the *Pacific Greenbacker* and the *Illustrated Graphic.*

To conclude his Address the Philosopher played lustily on the heartstrings of his readers: "Let us, therefore, cherish the recollections of that glorious past—these souvenirs of gallant deeds and grand achievements; and if, amid the thronging multitudes who seek fame and fortune in this favored land of

[2] Reprinted in *The Vidette,* organ of the Mexican War Veterans, Vol. 3, No. 9, June 15, 1882.

our acquirement, we are, in our waning years, and most of us impoverished, to be shoved aside and forgotten, let us console ourselves with the reflection that posterity will do us justice."[3]

Pickett was nearing his end. During 1881 he was perhaps incapacitated by illness, as we have no record of him in that year. We know that in 1882 he was working on a sort of autobiography. In January he wrote for the *Examiner* (quite in disregard of the advice he had given to Democrats to leave that paper alone) a lengthy reminiscence of his exploration trip of 1845 along Puget Sound.[4] Later, in a letter to the *Bulletin,* he told of Oregon and Sonoma days, and said, "I have been preparing of late some historical facts of importance and personal incidents in my forty years' sojourn west of the Rocky Mountains, intending to bring such out in book form."[5]

It is to be regretted that Pickett did not complete his autobiography in the vein of these two pieces, wherein he abjured politics and personal controversy in favor of ethnical and geographical notes; or, if he did complete it, that it is unknown to this day. He had been in the thick of things, and had known everyone.

He knew that his time was approaching. For at least ten years he had been suffering from an inter-

---

[3] P. 23.   [4] January 21, 1882.
[5] An undated clipping from the *San Francisco Bulletin,* entitled "A Pioneer Reminiscential," *ca.* 1882, in the California Historical Society collections.

nal disorder. In the autumn of 1882, while in Sacramento, he had a premonition of his death. Before leaving on a trip to Yosemite, he requested George T. Knox, a notary public, to take charge of his affairs in the event his fears should be confirmed. In Knox's hands he placed a package which, he said, held all his worldly goods, apart from the clothes on his back; he desired that after his death the contents be sent to his brother William in Tennessee.

Thereupon he boarded the southbound train for the San Joaquin Valley. At Madera he took the stagecoach for Yosemite. Since the mid-'seventies, when the first vehicle road was opened, the Valley had become a scenic attraction comparable to Niagara Falls. His fellow passengers were three globetrotting Englishmen from Liverpool who had crossed the continent for almost no other purpose than to see Yosemite. The end of the first day brought them to Clark's Big Tree Station, twenty-six miles from the Valley. The next day, with the station's proprietor, Henry Washburne, Pickett rode in a buckboard over a new road to Glacier Point. They arrived at sundown, and had to descend the trail to the Valley after nightfall on foot, guided by bright starlight and the white granite sand of the pathway.

Putting up at Barnard's Hotel, Pickett spent a week of easy promenading about the Valley. On November 3d, near the end of his stay, he penned a letter to the *Bulletin*. Politics and polemics entered not into this communication; the sole subject was Yosemite, its tourists and scenic wonders.

Another English tourist came in Saturday afternoon and left at daylight next morning. Like many others who come to the Yosemite and visit other notable places, he appeared to be traveling only to boast of having been to them. Said he spent one day in New York, one at Niagara Falls, one in Chicago, and one in San Francisco, and had seen everything of note. He inquired the distance to Mirror Lake, starting for it a-foot, refusing to hire guide or horse to visit other points; took the wrong road and had to return in half an hour to condescend to be put upon the right one.

Additional to scenic, the investigating mind desires to study the geological formations and speculate thereon. The most attractive feature to me is the grouping, sculpturing, and painting of these lofty escarpments. Snow fell here on the 16th of September, earlier than known before by several weeks. More of it, as well as rain, fell during the earlier days of October, but all soon melted, leaving the valley and roads hither dry, and the atmosphere of crystal clearness. Visitors here since the middle of September have witnessed what those for several weeks preceding did not—the tumbling waters of the lofty Yosemite Falls.

The next day, he boarded the stage for Merced. The road was bad and the passengers were severely shaken up. Pickett's old ailment became aggravated. In the little foothill mining town of Mariposa he had to leave the stage. He made his way to the hotel kept by Mrs. Jane Gallison. He felt deathly ill, and it was all that he could do to introduce himself as Philosopher Pickett. The good woman took him for a philosopher indeed. She put him straight to bed and sent for a doctor.

For a few days he held his own, thanks to her devoted care. He would allow no one else to tend him, and the poor woman's hotel business suffered while she waited on the stricken man night and day. The town's two physicians, Doctors Turner and Bell, were also in attendance

It was to no avail. Pickett grew weaker and weaker. His money was gone. With Mrs. Gallison as his amanuensis, he wrote to his friend John Currey, the former chief justice, in San Francisco, asking him to send money enough to pay the hotel bill. In his own feeble and indistinct hand, Pickett added a last postscript: "Am dying with hemorrhage of the bowels."

Then he remembered the letter he had written to the *Bulletin* from Yosemite. It had never been mailed, as he had intended to post it in Merced. Mrs. Gallison put it with the letter to Judge Currey, ready for the westbound stage.

On the morning of Thursday, November 16th, he asked Mrs. Gallison to sit beside him. For several hours he talked fluently and rationally, ranging far into the past, of his judicial and journalistic friends, and of his elder brother William in Tennessee. Patiently his good Samaritan listened to this last discourse. Then he lay exhausted. Death was very near.

The afternoon came on. Rain began to fall. He heard the outbound stage roll in. The horses were changed and away it went, bearing his letters to San Francisco. Shortly before two o'clock, he took the hands of Mrs. Gallison, who had not left his bedside since early morning, and drew them gently across his brow and face, as though to give expression to the gratitude he felt for her who had watched over him like a guardian angel. The good woman's tears fell on the pillow beside his weary head. With great effort he raised his hand and pointed up. "The Gate is open," he whispered, and then closed his eyes forever.

They buried Philosopher Pickett the next day in the public cemetery. Led by Mrs. Gallison, a handful of the hotel guests saw him to his grave. The only services were in compliance with a request made by Pickett before his death: a reading by Mrs. Gallison of Byron's misanthropic *Inscription on the Monument of a Newfoundland Dog.*

When the news reached San Francisco, Judge Currey headed a subscription list to repay Mrs. Gallison. A sum much larger than the entire bill, including the burial charges, was sent to her. The *Call* concluded its obituary note by saying, "His face was a familiar one on Montgomery Street, and he will be missed by many here who had a charitable feeling for him." The *Bulletin,* which for years he had alternately contributed to and flayed, published his last letter on the front page, under the heading, "An Autumnal Yosemite Trip: Philosopher Pickett's Last Letter, Written a Few Days Before His Death at Mariposa."

In Sacramento, Knox opened the package left with him and found that it contained seventy dollars in gold—three twenty-dollar pieces and one ten-dollar piece—tied in a white silk handkerchief. The little hoard was sent to Pickett's brother William, who two years later joined him in death. The *Record-Union* wrote his epitaph: "He was a prolific writer of pamphlets, and by those who knew him best was esteemed as an affable, upright and intelligent, but decidedly eccentric, gentleman."[6]

Today, sixty years later, the little foothill town of Mariposa is not much changed. The old white courthouse, built in the 'fifties, is still in daily use. The *Gazette*, which reported Pickett's demise, still makes its appearance. And the cemetery, on an oak-grown knoll to the north of the village, is lightly sprinkled with graves new and old. Of Philosopher Pickett's there remains no trace. He is one with the foothill earth.

---

[6] My account of Pickett's last days is based on the following sources: *Mariposa Gazette*, November 18, 1882; *San Francisco Call*, November 18, 1882; *Sacramento Record-Union*, November 18, 20, 1882; *San Francisco Bulletin*, November 24, 1882; Shuck, *op. cit.*, pp. 373–374.

EIGHT UNPUBLISHED LETTERS
WRITTEN BY CHARLES EDWARD PICKETT
TO EDWARD M. KERN AND WILLIAM HEATH DAVIS
OCTOBER, 1846–NOVEMBER, 1847
RELATING TO THE CONQUEST OF CALIFORNIA
BY THE UNITED STATES OF AMERICA

NOTE

The letters to Kern are printed from transcripts made from photostats of the original manuscripts in the Huntington Library, where they are calendared as FS 100–103. They are included herewith by permission of that institution. The Fort Sutter Papers, to which these letters belong, were accumulated by Kern while he was in command at the fort; they were acquired by Henry E. Huntington in 1921.

The letters to Davis are printed from transcripts made from the original manuscripts in the private collection of Robert Ernest Cowan. They are included with the permission of Mr. Cowan. He acquired them in the early years of this century direct from William Heath Davis.

LETTER OF PICKETT'S TO E. M. KERN

Unpublished Letters

[LETTER 1]

San Francisco
Mr. E. Kern
2d Oct. 1846
Dr Sir—

Will you be kind enough to send down the package of letters I left with you to be forwarded to Oregon—care Capt. Grimes this place. I presume your despatches will acquaint you of the news stirring here which is various and contradictory. Portsmouth and Congress will both perhaps leave soon [—in] a day or two. Mormons at law again and will be all disbanded soon. I am now on a jury, Branan [*sic*] debt. I cannot write more as my name is called.[1]

Yours respectfully,

Edward M. Kern, Esq.   C. E. PICKETT
Commander
Fort Sacramento
California

[LETTER 2]

Pueblo of San Jose
31st Oct. 1846
Dr Davis—

I did not arrive here till day before yesterday, where we found all quiet, with the exception of the misdoings of Weber and his *bear party*—the most of whom are a great set of scamps, and are creating much dissatisfaction here by reason of their lawless doings. They started

---

[1] Brannan had been brought into court by his fellow Mormons, charged with misappropriation of funds. He was discharged when two juries were unable to arrive at a verdict. Thus Pickett had the distinction of serving on the first jury in San Francisco.

off yesterday in search of more horses, saddles, etc.—one party to sweep the Contra Costa. This last I am truly sorry for, for if any part of California should be exempt from these demands and the presence of such a party as this, it ought to be the Contra Costa. The horses over there, what few have been left by the Indians, are in constant use by our countrymen, and amongst those the officers of our men of war, who have ever been welcome to use them.

This place is rather dull now, but few from the country in, as they fear to loose their saddles and horses or have none to come on. I was invited to a wedding dinner yesterday and fandango last night, which will continue today. No pretty girls here though plenty of accommodating ones.

Had you not better go over the Bay in order to guard *the fair one* whilst the bears are prowling in that neighborhood,—they will be certain to pay old daddy demijohn a visit.

I shall be down in a day or two, till then Adios.

Yours ever,

[*William Heath Davis*]   C. E. PICKETT

[LETTER 3]   Yerba Buena
Dec. 18th 1846

Dear Davis—

We have had stirring times since you left. The day the Savannah came over it was reported that a considerable body of Californians were in the vicinity, and an attack meditated on this place. Capt. Mervine—though a brave man—seems quite nervous about operations in this country since his defeat south,—and is all the time in a great figet—worse than a hen on a hot griddle. He has stationed many men and officers on shore, and ordered the citizens to form a volunteer corps for defense of the place; every one not acquainted with the California character being on the qui vive for a night attack. I however sleep very soundly as I know that they would not dare an attack even with a thousand men.

In seeming contradiction to any great fear of an attack, several small companies of scouts have been sent out in the neighborhood, badly armed. One of these left a few days since, with Judge Bartlett in command, and news has just reached [here] that he is a prisoner. Some men from the Pueblo report that José La Cruz Sanchez rancho is deserted except by some Indians, who told them that the Sanchez had made Bartlett prisoner, and gone they knew not where. They have lately become much incensed against Bartlett, on account of his interference in some of their business. One of them who lived at the Mission was made prisoner here for a day or two. All the Californians living about the Mission except two have gone off—so says a Mormonite this morning.

There is not much sympathy felt for Bartlett, as all think he had no business leaving town, particularly as his presence is all the time necessary in his office; it seems his wish I believe to have a finger in every pie.

Ridley returned this morning—unsuccessful in his search, having examined every part of the Bay as well as both rivers, without obtaining any clue to the boat. Some report came by an Indian a day or two since that they were prisoners, but this is not now believed.[2]

---

[2] The search was for the missing launch of the *Warren* and its twelve men, including two sons of Captain Montgomery. The boat

Jones has run down quite low, his last appearance on the stage being the evening we were organizing our company, which he was opposing by trying to start another, with himself at the head. During our meeting he raised his big speckled stick to strike Hyde, but was stopped by Mervine and Hull who got between them. We elected Howard captain but he declined serving, whereupon Smith was made captain. I might have got the command myself, but declined any such military honors.

We are all starved out in the way of beef, and Brown talks of closing house.

Dr. Jones I am told has bought or is bargaining for Fisher's brig.

Howard Oakley having no home to suit him to go to would perhaps have remained, but for getting jealous of me; and actually armed himself one night as I have since learned to shoot me, for trying to ———— his wife. I acknowledged the corn to him as she was fool enough to tell all—though against her will to do it; but excused myself by saying I merely wished to test the Mormon faith. The little fool has told it all about town; and says that he was quite easy after Longley left, whom he had strong suspicions of doing the same, and was compelled to watch him closely. He says there was great danger in staying here, as Mary was such a good easy creature, and

was dispatched late in November from Yerba Buena to New Helvetia, the officers having some business to transact with Kern, and perhaps carrying $900 with which to pay off the garrison. They never arrived at Sutter's, and no trace of the launch was ever found. It is likely that the sailors murdered the officers, destroyed the boat, and fled with the money. See Bancroft, *History of California*, V:384.

might have been crawled over, whilst he was on guard. I think he was very correct in this.

No news from your Dulcinea del Contra Costa de la Union.

Old Don Nathan has fenced up the lot in front of you, thereby cutting off your landing, and turning some trade from you; but I have opened a gangway, and I am feeding our little stove with the palings.

May good success attend you south. I am told wine is plenty at the Pueblo. Tell Longley not to forget my share.

Best respects to him and the little Captain.

Ever most truly yours,

[*William Heath Davis*]   CHAS. E. PICKETT

[LETTER 4]

Yerba Buena
11th Jany. 1847

Dear Davis—

Agreeably to contract, as well as the dictates of my own wishes, I have again the opportunity and pleasure of addressing you on the topics of general and private interests in our community. No pleasure in the news I give though. You may have gathered from my last letter that things were getting in a muss with us, and now I regret to add that the thing is too true. Yerba Buena is a perfect hell, all in a fever, the animosity and bad feeling of three or four different parties raging at once, and heaven only knows where the end will be. All law, justice and common sense has been thrown aside with us, and as a consequence, anarchy and misrule is reigning

supreme. Wherefore is this you will ask. I answer, because Capts. Mervine and Hull *both* and *neither* of
whom are in command here, are men of very weak intellect and no judgment. The whole of their operations
are conducted either through the blind random suggestions of their own minds, or directed by a set of ignorant
and knavish advisers, whom they have allowed to worm
and fawn themselves into their good graces and opinions. Some objected to Capt. Montgomery's administration, because he allowed certain improper things to
be done. But few of us here now of any correct thinking, but sadly regret his leaving and wish much for his
return.

Upon Bartlett's being taken prisoner, Hyde, against
the wishes of a majority here who suspected his character, was appointed Alcalde in his stead; and his high
handed, ignorant and illegal acts thus far in his short
official career, have but too well justified the suspicions
entertained against him.

Bartlett's acts, though objected to in some instances,
were wisdom and purity compared with those of his
successor. Hyde has in fact proved himself an *unprincipled villain;* and if hereafter, when this military power,
around which he had parasitically clung, and grown to
an ephemeral consequence, shall be withdrawn from the
land and his support—I do not prove him such, then let
all the punishment and odium which he would deserve
were he guilty fall on my head.

The war has begun and ended here since you left.
Some rumours were prevalent in town about six weeks
since of a party of Californians in this vicinity, and great

preparations made to prevent an attack on the town, which was kept in a constant ferment and state of alarm, the soldiers and citizens being round up for battle nearly every night by Grannies Mervine and Hull, who have not slept 6 nights for that time. And although such fears were felt for the safety of the place yet small parties were constantly going out to the Mission and beyond. Bartlett with six men went to the Mission, where he danced all night and next day proceeded to Sanchez with his Baqueros for cattle, and whilst in the act of surrounding a band of beeves in the prairie, was pounced on by the Californians and made prisoner together with all his men. Our efficient commanders here did not stir a soldier to go in pursuit, and not till nearly three weeks after, and until the arrival of Capt. Weber here with a party of 35 men, was a force organized under Capt. Marston to go out. Capt. Bailar Smith, with volunteers from Yerba Buena, together with Weber and Marston's company, composed a force of about 100 men.

These proceeded—having one cannon, which was a great bore and trouble—on the track of the enemy, whom they found in the woods just this side of Santa Clara. At the time the fight commenced Weber and Smith were absent scouting with a few men each but managed on hearing the firing to get back safely. But such a battle! O shades of Alexander and Bounaparte! hide your faces whilst it is told. The Californians were 120 in all, mounted on good horses, which they took good care should keep them out of the range of the shot, which caused our forces to waste a vast deal of ammunition to no purpose. Finding nothing could be done there, our army marched on towards the Mission, the Californians, surrounding them in the mustard on every side, and presenting only a single man in a spot to be fired at, each exchanging shot at from a quarter to a half mile distant. A halt was ordered every few hundred yards, when a broadside was blazed away; doing considerable damage to the mustard stalks. When the cannon was to be fired, a man would mount on it, sight with his hand the direction of the enemy, when jumping down, off she was banged. The result of the day's fight was two men on our side got a slight scratch one not drawing blood, and one killed and two badly wounded on the other side.

Preparations were about being made by the volunteers to go and attack their camp that night, but a flag of truce came in and demanded an armistice, proposing terms of treaty, provided their grievances were redressed.

A courier was instantly sent here to learn Capt. Hull's orders, which on arrival at Santa Clara, formed a basis for a treaty of peace. The Californians to lay down their arms, deliver up what horses they had taken and go quietly home, being promised justice and good treatment hereafter. The Americans to deliver up what horses belonged to them. This last however occasioned a great row among our own folks, and came very near producing a bloody and unhappy termination amongst them.

It seems that Capt. Marston, whom all calm and sensible persons must admit, was actuated by the kindest and best of motives, lacked energy, judgment and decision, in settling the preliminaries of the treaty, and in giving nothing more than proper justice to the Californians. As the latter, (which was composed of all the rascals and scurf in the country—but three respectable men in the ranks besides their leaders, the Sanchez)—took advantage of Marston's kind intentions and strict adherence to the articles of the treaty, and commenced claiming and lassoing horses that did not belong to them—setting nearly all Weber's men afoot in doing so; as they would put their ropes on the horses with the riders on them, who were compelled to dismount and unsaddle. In this way horses were taken that did not belong to them and carried into the Pueblo and sold for two or three dollars, before the owner could reclaim them.

The day after the truce commenced Lieut. Maddox from Monterey arrived with 60 men and he took sides with Weber against Marston in the settlement of the treaty and exchange of horses. There matters stood—Maddox, Weber and the volunteers generally except those from here, on one side, and Marston, Forbes and Dr. Duval on the other, and poor Bartlett also I believe, but so broken down and cowed that he had but little to say.

After this was over and the Californians exulting at their success, for they not only got horses that did not belong to them, but also kept some of their best arms,—Sanchez excusing this by saying that the men ran off with them whilst the treaty was going on, which was the fact, as they were seen going but whether by connivance of Sanchez or not is left to conjecture. Maddox required 15 saddles to mount some volunteers going to return with him. The Californians refused to surrender, saying they could not go home as they had promised if these were taken from them. Maddox insisted, the Californians got angry and pretended they would fight again—though having no arms—when Marston seeing another row, and supposing his absence in the excited state of affairs might be beneficial, left for the Embarcadero. The saddles were taken, when Dr. Duval started immediately for Marston and got an order for their restoration to the owners. On presenting this some high words ensued between him and Maddox, the latter accusing him of meddling in business that did not concern him. Duval resented this by telling him he was ready to answer to him personally for any insult or affront he conceived had been offered him, and would interfere when it pleased him wherever his inclination or duty called him. Maddox and Forbes—the latter having been the mutual friend and negotiator in the treaty—also had a warm set to. Forbes accusing him of staining the honor of the American flag, and compromising the honor and faith of Capt. Marston and himself (Forbes).

Maddox at length said he would take the saddles on to the Pueblo, where if he got some from Weber, these would be given up.

Smith and his company with Duval and Bartlett then came off and arrived here yesterday (Sunday) and Capt. Marston at night in the boats. Thus ended the present campaign in the Northern District. When it commences again I will send you a bulletin.

I am just informed that the wounded men on our side were not touched by the enemy, as they at first supposed and so reported, but hurt themselves in the oak bushes. And it is even doubted whether the Californians recd. any injury. The fight lasted several hours. And the treaty which was made half way between the Mission and the oaks, in sight of the two armies, lasted nearly one whole day.

A Devil of a rumpus is kicked up about the first issue from the Star office. Hull is much incensed in reference to the two articles signed Yerba Buena—called on Jones for the author, who told him it was me, and required the editor to apologize in his next paper for inserting such articles. Jones has talked pretty plainly to the Capt., rather daring him to interfere with the liberty of the press, and has written him a note in reference to the course [upon which] he (Hull) expects his paper shall be conducted, intimating that no apology is to be given, and that $5000 per month is to be charged to the U. States in case it is ordered to be stopped. Hull also objected to other matter, or rather his advisers do for him. The poor man is in a perfect fever and wants to leave; he says he does not know what his authority is here, as he is styled Commander of Northern District of California, Gov., etc., but finds that Mervine takes all command when he pleases. In fact nobody here, neither officers, soldiers nor citizens, know who is in command. Nor do we know what rules, laws, regulations, etc., we are governed by, the Alcalde doing as he pleases, and Hull sanctioning all.

They are full of lawsuits both at Sonoma and the Pueblo as well as here; and great opposition and bad feeling in respect to the way law is administered. The fact is, I begin to think that José La Cruz Sanchez' prophecy will be true about our fighting amongst ourselves, which you recollect he made at the time he asked you about going to the Islands on the brig. All the volunteers up this way are more than ever opposed to the Navy officers having anything to do with them.

Those about the Pueblo, whose time will be out soon, say that unless a better state of command is not placed here, that none will enlist again, and if any necessity exist for an armed force, they will act on their own hook in the business. In this place we are all so worried and disgusted at the state of affairs for some weeks past, that if the vote were put tomorrow for every officer and soldier of the Navy to go aboard and stay there, and let us get 25 volunteers in the barracks, it would carry by a large majority.

I would mention in reference to the California army— that most of them say they were forced into it by the Sanchez. Francisco Sanchez says that he started the whole, and did it in protection for his property against Bartlett and Leidesdorff, as also to oppose Weber's treatment of the same, who have gained great enmity from the natives around here. They had no flag, and denied being at all Mexican. This story about the affair was told soon after B. was taken, and a trap was laid, 'tis said, to get Leidesdorff also whom they would have shot.

I think, and so does he too, fearing to sleep in his house on acct. of being murdered or taken

[The rest of the letter is lacking]

[*William Heath Davis*]

[LETTER 5]

Yerba Buena
Jan. 14, 1847

Dear Kern—

Your favor of the 5th is at hand, and I am sorry my mind is not as free from trouble as yours, in order to answer you in the same humorous strain. We are in a perfect ferment, and ready for *mutiny* or anything else to change the present state of affairs, and get rid of our web-footed rulers, who are about as much fitted for the command they have on shore in this country, as a porpoise, or the horse that one of the tyrants of old times, made governor of a province.

You thought Montgomery not the best man in the world for Commander and Gov. of the Northern District of California,—but he was a General and Statesman compared with the two brainless bipeds now holding his command. I say the two, for a sort of duumvirate now exists. Hull has the title, but Old Mervine is ashore half his time ordering and directing, and many warm and animated debates is had daily amongst citizens, as well as officers, as to who is Commander. In fact both Hull and Mervine themselves, confess they don't know (which does not in the least surprise me) who ought to be head—Mervine ranking him in the navy. So to compromise matters, they take it turn about, Hull doing all the small jobs, that Mervine does not happen to notice, or care for attending to.

The Sanchez and Bartlett war is over, the former asserting that, he and his friends were merely on their own hook, to defend their cattle and other property from being stolen, by *Uncle Sam's high minded and chivalrous* officers and citizens. They had no flag, and I doubt not what they say; and glory in their spunk.

The volunteers at the Pueblo talk of no longer heeding any commands from him, having been worried and disgusted to such a degree; and if necessary for defense will set up a garrison at Santa Clara on their own hook.

I have not room to write you all the infernal rascally ignorant illegal and high handed proceedings on the part of our civil and military men here. I only assert, and will prove it hereafter that our flag has been stained with dishonor and our temple of justice degraded and prostituted to the lowest depths of infamy and disgrace. The only consolation in all this is that they have got by the ears themselves. A great rumpus was kicked up at the surrender of Sanchez's army (worse by far, they say, than old Falstaff's) between our folks and a bloody termination mighty near happening. 'Tis not all over yet.

Jones and myself are expecting to be challenged every day, or swung to the yard arm, only for insulting our officers and the navy generally.

Old Hull demanded the author of the pieces signed "Yerba Buena," and on learning it was me, told Jones he must *issue a paper next day in order to apologize.* O cracky! Jones told him he would consider on it, has written Old Hull a note about interfering with the liberties of the press etc., and put the poor weak soul in a peck of trouble, he curses the lawyers all to hell, and says they make the whole of the trouble and disturbance.

I suspect from the tone of your letter (and am sorry for you) that some fair one has been unkind, and not presented front to meet your bayonet charge. Don't despair old fellow, but at 'em again! "better luck next time"—"no use in crying"—Why don't you rent that barren field up there and try whether your seed will sprout, as I know the soil is quite anxious to fructify and raise a crop. In fact you will be defended by our preemption laws in *jumping* the whole claim, as the original settler on it, has probably abandoned it and stuck his stake elsewhere.

Yours ever,

C. E. PICKETT

P.S. As for that $10, you need not trouble yourself to put it in your report now, as I mentioned your receipting it for me, only because I was a little vexed at the time in being so treated about what government owes me $300, which I much wanted. The sum is too trifling to cause any derangement in your accounts by crediting now.

C. E. P.

My respects to Mrs. Montgomery and the rest of the folks.

Capt. E. Kern
Ft. Sacramento
A. C.

[LETTER 6]

Yerba Buena
20th Jany. 1847

Dear D.—

An opportunity is just at hand to send you the enclosed sheets.

Things are going on here as when I wrote these, only a little more so. The devil has full sway at present, using a parcel of "Blue bellied Yankees" "dyed in the wool" "clothed with a little brief authority" as his agents and tools.

The only consolation to all honest and good citizens is that these fellows have already taken enough of rope to hang themselves, and will sure to be swung, if ever truth be told, or justice be done them for their lawless misdeeds here. Heaven grant their day of trial may come soon that we may get rid of such an infernal state of affairs.

Sherman has managed everything well and actively since you left, except turning the room adjoining mine into a shoe shop. This I should not mention to you, but for my repeated intimations to him of the impropriety of such a thing, and the assertion that I knew it was a thing you would be displeased at. He has had Howard Oakley hammering and stitching away here for weeks, every day and sometimes nights, to the great boring and inconvenience of myself as well as Cooper and the Kanakas. You wished me to pay attention and do the civilities to your gentlemen customers; but I cannot ask them back to take a warm or sit and smoke or drink, because the place is filled up with benches, lasts, leather, dirt, etc. Some have stopped calling for this very reason. And we are bothered often by persons hunting around with old boots and shoes enquiring for the shoemaker's shop, which they learned was kept at Davis store. I don't think this sounds well, as it is not calculated to make your establishment a fashionable resort or draw to you the better sort of customers. And I have told Sherman I would rather help to build the man a house if he were not able to get one, rather than suffer him here.

We are to have a ball two nights hence, when I expect to see the lovely one from over the bay, as a boat goes for them tomorrow. What shall I say for you.

Sherman and myself belong to the liberal independent party here, which is at present a little under par, although we are in the majority, both amongst our fellow citizens as well as officers of the navy. Some in the latter whom you admire most are on our side, but are compelled to have their tongues tied. I would mention Fauntleroy, Carter, Tansill—though you don't know the last—and some other of the younger ones. Ward, Howard, Mellus, Leidsdorff and Hyde, his man Friday, with some few others of less note belong to the other party.

A Russian brig from Sitka is in after wheat.

I hope to see you up soon. Bring me some law books from Monterey.

Yours truly,

C. E. PICKETT

Wm. H. Davis
Brig Euphemia
Monterey or south

[LETTER 7]

San Fran. Cal.
14 — Feby. 1847

Dear Capt.—

Your much esteemed, but unreadable favor got to hand in due time, and I return it that you may write it over for me; as I always wish to preserve for my children the correspondence of their pop with his old friends.

Everything is still disjointed and helter skelter and nobody as yet knows whether martial law is in force or not. The tories and Hullites or more properly Hellites,

are a little flustrated at the idea of their Catspaw leaving
with his ship in a few days. The villains will be put to
it to get another official tool to work their iniquitous
schemes with. And strange to say they seem to be ignorant of the mine and magazine they themselves have
placed under their feet, which is destined ere long to
blow them all to hell.

Lieut. Tansill now in command here is a free, liberal
and intelligent fellow—a genuine one I assure you. And
from the first landing in California from the Dale, he
has denounced the mad and high handed schemes carried on here by his brother officers, as does everybody
else of sense and honesty. The late organization and
appointment of officers, has given disgust and created
a bitter spirit of opposition to the acts of Stockton and
crew, throughout the land than yet felt and you know
it was bad enough before. Even Stockton's friends in
the navy are now out against him, and say that he is
mad, crazy, and beside himself. Bryant and Hastings
got up yesterday from below, and represent all Fremont's army and every foreigner down there, to be in
no very amiable mood. Indeed but little more and the
web footed gentry would be ordered from the country
and have to leave nolens volens.

What a Godsend if this had been done five months
ago. Poor California and some brave lives lost would,
had this been, be now rejoicing under the peaceable
and protecting care of the Star spangled banner.

Tell my and your magisterial friend, that like most
other men from his section of our Union he is quite
ignorant of the stuff that's in a man of genuine prin-

ciples, and of the deeds he would dare do and the risk run, in opposing tyranny and falsehood. Say to him that is but a sprinkling of what I have done to some of these petty scoundrels here, that I have told them to their teeth of their rascality, have written some flaming articles whilst in my prison denouncing the whole fraternity and their wrong course, but which Jones would not publish. Tell him I would not only dare all the power of man, the devil and hell in opposing falsehood and giving utterance to truth; but would march boldly to the very throne of the Great Jehovah, and demand justice and the sway of right.

I see two ships of war in this morning, the Erie and Cyane, I suppose. The Savannah will go today.

I wish you and Sutter, as you have but little else to do, to write me all about the Indians of the Sacramento and San Joaquin, their population, number of rancheros—the way they have ever behaved themselves and been treated by the whites. All the particulars about Fremont's massacre, together with a rough map of the country—size of the valley—proportion of Tula—barren plain, hills, good arable land etc. Also length of Sacramento and other rivers. Mark the distances on the map and all the names well.

Tell Peter Assiniboine I wish him to send me that map of South Oregon he promised.

Send me down some of your drawings for copying samples.

Are you in the line of promotion, civil or military. You talk of leaving Othello's occupation. I think you are right, it is not suitable to your genius, and besides it is too much disgraced here now for a man of your mould to damn himself in. I am so disgusted with the low scheming cunning and trickery by our shirt tail out mountebank office seekers—that nothing insults me more [than] for a man to tell me I am after an office and I am vexed to think I can't get one. As to getting one the people of this place will elect me to any I want that's in their power to give, but I would scorn to be caught in such a lousy ignorant crowd as are now officiating. God help poor California.

You will yet learn who the editor of the Star[8] is if you don't believe me when I tell you he is the very worst and most dangerous man in all California; an unprincipled schemer and plotter of the same order but worse in character than Machiavelli. His whole soul is devoted to making money and gaining fame and political preferment; to do this he would trample on the neck of friends, father and brothers. Why think you he won't publish any communications? Do you take?

Yours ever,
C. E. PICKETT

P.S. I send you some paper to write on.

How do you like the appointment of your friends Russell and Larkin. Thought you would have been sorry, though you have not yet studied sufficiently the art of soft soaping and backside licking to get California offices.

E. M. Kern, Esq.

---

[8] I.e., E. P. Jones.

[LETTER 8]

San Francisco, California
12th Nov. 72 A.R. [1847]

My Dear Kern—

I write this with the hope that you are still in Monterey—as you have it in your power to go by a better,
shorter, quicker and cheaper route than your present
proposed or *unproposed* one.

Judge Thornton has just arrived from Oregon on his
way to Washington. The bark Whiton on which he
came down stays here ten days or two weeks and then
goes direct to Mazatlan. From thence to Panama are
frequent conveyances—but to ensure a passage quickly
on [them], the Judge as also Capt. Folsom for him writes
to Governor Mason by this mail to offer himself as a
bearer of dispatches home, which if assented to, will give
him some authority to require of our Naval Commander at Mazatlan to facilitate his journey onward by
sending a vessel especially for this purpose, should none
be sailing soon.

Even should Governor Mason decline transmitting
documents—you run but little risk of detention going
this route, as the Commodore on that station frequently
sends down to get the mails. In view of your going in
the Whiton I intended seeing Capt. Gelston about the
passage money, but he is not ashore today. Judge Thornton, however thinks it will not be over fifty dollars to
M., which is a very fair price. If you conclude to change
berths, one of you had better come up immediately to
make the bargain with Capt. G. about calling in at

Monterey for your baggage and the rest of your company. Toler and family will also go I presume.

I received some very unlooked for news from Oregon; that I have been appointed Indian Agent for that Territory. The number of the Star I send you acquaints you with my intentions in the matter. There is a very false and abusive article in a number of the Oregon Spectator respecting my appointment, but I am well aware from what clique that comes; and this party inimical to me there has control of the paper. 'Tis not because of any opposition in Oregon to my filling the office, that I decline accepting, as the selection of any citizen in the Terry. who has resided there as long as myself—even were he as wise as King Solomon, as pure and good as Jesus Christ and as brave as Julius $\begin{cases} \text{Caesar} \\ \text{Cesar} \\ \text{Cezar} \\ \text{Caezar} \end{cases}$?

would have been met in the same spirit. But I have several other and weighty objections to taking this post, of which you shall be made acquainted in time.

Should this find you in Monterey, and you decline going via Mazatlan, but continue on in the Shubrick[4] (God knows where!) you can inform the President or Walker of my resolve, provided my letters to them I shall send by Judge Thornton, do not get to Washington before you.

Ask Mr. Toler if he received a letter I wrote him a week or two since, making inquiries respecting some

---

[4] Kern had already left Monterey in the *Commodore Shubrick*, which of course Pickett did not know.

of my relatives, of whom I presumed he had some knowledge; and you or him send me an answer to it, in order that I may avail myself, of such information as can be given, in writing home by Judge Thornton.

I am in the habit of copying all my letters before they are fit to be sealed and sent off. The face of this however shows it to be an exception to this rule. I am not in the habit of making such schoolboy-excuses as this but an apology is certainly due here.

I look for the letter you promised from Monterey daily.

Yours ever,

C. E. PICKETT

P.S. To Major King and Roubideau my kindest love and respects go.

E. M. Kern, Esq.
Care Mr. Longley
Monterey, A. C.

Biographical Repertory of the Pickett Letters

ASSINIBOINE, PETER
  Probably an Assiniboine Indian guide.
BARTLETT, WASHINGTON ALLEN
  Lieutenant on the *Portsmouth*. First American alcalde of San
  Francisco, who changed its name from Yerba Buena. Born in
  Maine, *ca.* 1820, died 1871. Not to be confused with Washington
  Bartlett (1824–1887), who arrived in San Francisco in 1849 from
  Georgia and became successively newspaper publisher, mayor of
  San Francisco, and governor of California.
BRANNAN, SAMUEL
  New York state printer and Mormon elder, arrived in Yerba
  Buena July 31, 1846, aboard the *Brooklyn,* as leader of some 230
  co-religionists. Later prominent as merchant and capitalist. Took
  to drink, and after many vicissitudes died at Escondido, San
  Diego County, in 1889.
BROWN, JOHN HENRY
  Native of Devonshire, prominent in San Francisco from 1846 to
  1850 as a hotelkeeper. In 1886 he published his "Reminiscences"
  of those early days. Died in Santa Cruz, 1905, at the age of 94.
BRYANT, EDWIN
  . Native of Massachusetts. Made several trips to California. His
  What I Saw in California is an authority on the events of 1846–47.
  Died at Louisville, Kentucky, in 1869, at the age of 64.
CARTER, JOSEPH O.
  A Honolulu merchant; at one time a partner of W. H. Davis in
  San Francisco.
COOPER, JOHN
  An Englishman known as "Jack the Soldier." Lived with his wife
  on a fifty-vara lot at the intersection of Jackson and Kearny
  streets. According to John Henry Brown, he was a regular Jack-
  of-all-trades and worked at whatever he could find to do.
DAVIS, WILLIAM HEATH
  Born at Honolulu in 1822. First visited California in 1831. From
  1845 onward was a San Francisco merchant and shipowner. Died
  at Hayward in 1909. His *Seventy-five Years in California* was
  published posthumously.

DUVAL, MARIUS

Assistant surgeon on the *Portsmouth;* acting lieutenant in Stockton's battalion, 1846–47.

FAUNTLEROY, DAINGERFIELD

A Virginian, born in 1799. Purser in the U.S. Navy for many years. Captained a company of volunteer dragoons who kept order in the Monterey district, July-September, 1846. Died at Pensacola Navy Yard in 1853.

FOLSOM, JOSEPH

Graduate of West Point; came to California as captain in U.S. Army. Made a fortune in San Francisco town-lot speculation. Died at Mission San Jose, aged 38.

FORBES, JAMES ALEXANDER

A Scotchman who came to California in 1831. From 1841 he acted as British vice-consul. Died at Oakland in 1881, at the age of 77.

GELSTON, ROLAND

Master of the bark *Whiton* and a San Francisco merchant in 1847–49.

GRIMES, ELIAB

Trader and merchant of Honolulu and San Francisco. Died in 1848 at the age of 69.

HASTINGS, LANSFORD WARREN

Early pioneer, promoter, Mormon agent. Practiced law in San Francisco in 1847–48. He died about 1870.

HOWARD, WILLIAM DAVIS MERRY

Pioneer trader of San Francisco, in partnership with Henry Mellus. Died in 1856, at the age of 37.

HULL, JOSEPH BARTINE

Commander of the *Warren;* in command at San Francisco, 1846–47.

HYDE, GEORGE

Second American alcalde of San Francisco, generally unpopular.

JONES, ELBERT P.

Kentuckian, lawyer, first editor of the *Star.* Died at Charleston, South Carolina, in 1852.

KERN, EDWARD M.

Born at Philadelphia in 1823. Came to California in 1845 as artist and topographer with the Frémont expedition. From the outbreak of the Bear Flag Revolt he commanded the garrison at New Helvetia, much to Sutter's annoyance. He started east with Stockton in 1847, but was left behind ill, and sailed from San Francisco in October of the same year on the *Shubrick.* The

Kern River and Kern County are named after him. He died at Philadelphia in 1863. See H. A. Spindt's "Notes on the Life of Edward M. Kern," Kern County Historical Society, *Annual Publication No. 5*, November, 1939.

KING, HENRY

One of Frémont's party, who served as captain and commissary of the California Battalion, and went east on the *Shubrick* in October, 1847. Joining Frémont's fourth expedition in 1848, he was frozen to death and probably eaten by his companion. Apparently a brother of James King of William.

LARKIN, THOMAS OLIVER

Came to California in 1832 as a trader, settled in Monterey. Served as first (and only) United States consul. Died at San Francisco in 1858.

LEIDESDORFF, WILLIAM ALEXANDER

Arrived in 1841 in command of the schooner *Julia Ann;* became American vice-consul at San Francisco in 1845 by appointment by Consul Larkin. He died in 1848.

LONGLEY, WILLIAM RUFUS

Came from Honolulu, on the *Euphemia,* as clerk for W. H. Davis, in 1846–47.

MADDOX, WILLIAM

Lieutenant on the *Cyane* and *Congress.* Took part in the Sanchez campaign.

MARSTON, WARD

Captain of marines on the *Savannah;* in command of San Francisco garrison and force that marched to Santa Clara against Sanchez.

MASON, RICHARD BARNES

Colonel of the 1st U.S. Dragoons, who reached California in 1847, serving as governor from May of that year until February, 1849. Died of cholera in St. Louis in 1849 or 1850.

MELLUS, HENRY

Came to California in 1835 before the mast with Dana on the *Pilgrim.* In 1845 formed a partnership with W. D. M. Howard, and their firm became the most prominent in San Francisco merchandising. Died at Los Angeles in 1860.

MERVINE, WILLIAM

Commander in the U.S. Navy, in charge of the landing party at Monterey, July 7, 1846, when the American flag was raised. Defeated by the Californians while attempting to march from San Pedro to Los Angeles.

MONTGOMERY, JOHN BERRIEN
Commander of the *Portsmouth,* who first raised the American flag in San Francisco, July 9, 1846. Later in command of Charlestown Navy Yard. Died in 1873.

OAKLEY, HOWARD
One of the Mormon immigrants of 1846; a member of the third Donner relief party.

RIDLEY, ROBERT
English sailor and clerk, arrived at San Francisco in 1840. Captain of the port in 1846, and second alcalde. Died at the Misión San Francisco de Asís, in 1851.

ROUBIDEAU, ANTOINE
A mountain man, who came with Kearny in 1846 as guide. Generally spelled Robidoux.

RUSSELL, WILLIAM H.
Politician and lawyer.

SANCHEZ, FRANCISCO
Native Californian owner of the San Pedro ranch near San Francisco. Aroused by repeated theft of his livestock by the United States forces, he and his brother José de la Cruz seized Alcalde Bartlett and thus precipitated the Santa Clara campaign.

SHERMAN, RICHARD M.
Employee of W. H. Davis. Later a merchant and property owner.

SMITH, BAILAR
Possibly a nickname of the following Smith, to whom Pickett is clearly referring.

SMITH, WILLIAM M.
Former circus rider, San Francisco merchant, captain of volunteers in the Santa Clara campaign. Took to drink and committed suicide in 1854.

NATHAN, DON [i.e., "DON" NATHAN SPEAR]
Trader in the Islands and California. In 1836 he formed a partnership with Leese & Hinckley to open a store in San Francisco. Uncle and original employer of William Heath Davis. Died at San Francisco in 1849 at the age of 47.

STOCKTON, ROBERT FIELD
Commander of the *Congress* and of the Pacific Squadron. Military governor of California until January, 1847. Died in 1866 at the age of 70.

TANSILL, ROBERT
Lieutenant of marines on the *Dale.* Commander of the San Francisco garrison in 1847.

THORNTON, JESSY QUINN

Oregon pioneer lawyer who touched at San Francisco in November, 1847, on his way east by sea. He later published *Oregon and California in 1848*. While in Oregon he served as a justice of the Oregon Supreme Court.

TOLER, WILLIAM P.

Midshipman on the *Savannah*.

WARD, JAMES C.

Prominent in San Francisco trading and politics in 1847–48. Died in 1883.

WEBER, CHARLES M.

Arrived in 1841. Worked for Sutter. Served as alcalde of San Jose. Took part in Santa Clara campaign. Founded town of Stockton, where he died in 1881 at the age of 67.

Bibliography

PICKETT'S PUBLICATIONS

Address of Charles E. Pickett to the California Legislature, upon the Government Fee in the Public Domain—Intercommunication and Land Monopolies and Correlative Topics. [Sacramento, 1874] 16 pp.

Address to the Veterans of the Mexican War. Embodying a historical contrast of the two great political parties of the United States, on vital issues, with personal reminiscences and other pertinent episodes; also an appendix of three chapters entitled "The California Democratic State Club Pilloried"; "A New Plundercrat Organ Disguised in the Garb of Democracy"; "To the Greenback-Labor Voters." By Charles Edward Pickett. M.W.V. and Pacific Coast Pioneer of 1842. [San Francisco, September, 1880] 28 pp.

American Education Analyzed; or, a Synoptical Disquisition on the Quality, Culture, Development, Rank and Government of Man. With an addendum describing the order of men to select for office. By Charles Edward Pickett. San Francisco, 1877. 46 pp.

The California King: His Conquests, Crimes, Confederates, Counsellors, Courtiers and Vassals. Stanford's Post-Prandial New-Year's Day Soliloquy. [San Francisco, 1876] 15 pp. [Issued anonymously]

The Existing Revolution, Its Causes and Results. By Charles Edward Pickett. Sacramento, 1861. 24 pp. [Second edition, same year, same pagination, has one page of added matter]

Flumgudgeon Gazette and Bumble Bee Budget: A Newspaper of the Salmagundi Order, Devoted to Scratching and Stinging the Follies of the Times. Edited by the Curltail Coon. Volume I, Number 8, August 20, 1845. [Manuscript newspaper written pseudonymously by Pickett *circa* June–August, 1845, at Oregon City, Oregon, during the session of the Legislative Committee. Approximately a dozen copies issued biweekly]

Gwinism in California. N.p., n.d. [1860] 8 pp.

John C. Fremont, His Character, Achievements, and Qualifications for the Presidency; and Other Matters Connected Therewith. By Chas. E. Pickett. N.p. [Sacramento? 1856] 16 pp.

Land-Gambling versus Mining-Gambling: An Open Letter to Squire P. Dewey, Relative to His Participation in the Land-Gambling of San Francisco in Early Days. From One Who Knows.

[Preface and text signed C. E. Pickett.] Second edition, with additions. San Francisco, November, 1879. 24 pp. [First edition not located]

Land-Gambling vs. Mining-Gambling. Third edition, containing an open letter each to Chief Justice Waite and Ex-U.S. Attorney-General Speed; also a chapter entitled "Fieldiana." With all the matter of the second edition. San Francisco, February, 1880. 40 pp.

A Letter from Charles E. Pickett to Jno. A. Eagan, Secretary of the Amador Miners' League, and Other Matter. San Francisco, August 12th, 1871. 8 pp.

Oration Delivered in the Congregational Church, Sacramento, California, July 4, 1857. By Charles Edward Pickett. San Francisco, Whitton, Towne & Co.'s Excelsior Steam Presses, 1857. 32 pp.

A Pamphlet for the Times! Containing an Address of C. E. Pickett to the Settlers of California, Their Platform of Principles, and Other Matter, Showing the Workings in This State of Broderick-Biglerism. [San Francisco, June 25th, 1855] 16 pp.

The Paris Exposition and Other Expositions. By Charles Edward Pickett. Some leaves from the life of a Pacific Slope pioneer of 1842. San Francisco, 1877. 15 pp.

Petition of Charles E. Pickett. Document No. 45 in Appendix to Journal of the 4th Session of the Legislature of the State of California. San Francisco, George Kerr, State Printer, 1853. 4 pp.

Philosopher Pickett's Anti-Plundercrat Pamphlet. Dedicated to the Partially Disenthralled People of California. San Francisco, June, 1879. 74 pp.

Pickett's Pamphlet on the Railway, Chinese, and Presidential Questions. San Francisco, Cal., May, 1876. 24 pp.

Protest and Memorial against Granting Appropriation to the Immigrant Aid Society. [Sacramento, T. A. Springer, State Printer, 1872] 5 pp.

Repudiation, Supreme Judges and the Newspapers. By Charles E. Pickett. [San Francisco, August, 1857] 8 pp.

The Western American. Vol. 1, No. 1, January 15, 1852 to Vol. 1, No. 32, March 1, 1852. San Francisco, Pickett & Co., Proprietors; Charles E. Pickett, Editor.

Pickett's seventeen pamphlets have not survived in great numbers; in fact, they are to be considered as rare items. This is not surprising when we bear in mind that the original printings, issued at the author's expense, were sharply limited by his impecuniosity.

He often included notices in them, giving the price of wholesale quantities and stating that he was keeping the type standing in anticipation of orders. It is fairly certain that no orders were ever received, at least not for wholesale quantities.

The list given above probably represents all of Pickett's published writings. In his pamphlets occur cross references to others of his works; none are mentioned which have not been located, except for a printed handbill which he says he issued, *Memorial to the California Legislature upon the Policy of Licensing and Regulating Gambling and Bawdy Houses,* and a printed prospectus for his newspaper, the *Western American.*

Today no library has all the original pamphlets. The University of California, Los Angeles, has the only complete collection of Pickett's writings, part of which are in photostat and on film. The California State Library, the University of California Library, Berkeley, the Bancroft Library, and the Huntington Library are the only other institutions that have more than two or three items.

Pickett's manuscripts are also rare, in spite of the fact that he probably wrote more essays, articles, and letters than any of his contemporaries. The Oregon Historical Society, the Bancroft Library, the California State Library, the State archives in Sacramento, the Huntington Library, and the private collection of Robert Ernest Cowan contain examples, all of which have been used or printed in this study.

Works Cited or Otherwise Drawn Upon

ALTER, J. C.
  James Bridger, Trapper, Frontiersman, Scout and Guide. Salt Lake City, Shepard Book Co., 1925.
APPLEGATE, JESSE, and APPLEGATE, JESSE A.
  A Day with the Cow Column in 1843. Recollections of My Boyhood. Edited by Joseph Schafer. Chicago, The Caxton Club, 1934.
BAGLEY, C. E.
  Early Catholic Missions in Old Oregon. Seattle, 1932.
BANCROFT, HUBERT HOWE
  California inter Pocula. San Francisco, The History Co., 1888.
  History of California. San Francisco, The History Co., 1884–90.
  History of Oregon. San Francisco, The History Co., 1890.
BATES, JOSEPH CLEMENT
  History of the Bench and Bar of California. San Francisco, Bench and Bar Publishing Co., 1912.

BOGGS, WILLIAM M.

W. M. Boggs' Manuscript about Bent's Fort, Kit Carson, the Far West, and Life among the Indians. Edited by Leroy R. Hafen. *In* The Colorado Magazine, March 1930.

BROWN, JAMES HENRY

Political History of Oregon. Provisional Government. Portland, Lewis & Dryden, 1892.

BROWN, JOHN HENRY

Reminiscences and Incidents of Early Days of San Francisco (1845–50). With an introduction and reader's guide by Douglas S. Watson. San Francisco, The Grabhorn Press, 1933.

BRYANT, EDWIN

What I Saw in California ... 1846–47. Edited by Marguerite E. Wilbur. Santa Ana, The Fine Arts Press, 1936.

BURNETT, PETER H.

Recollections & Opinions of an Old Pioneer. New York, Appleton & Co., 1880.

CAHN, FRANCES, and BARY, VALESKA

Welfare Activities of Federal, State, and Local Governments in California, 1850–1934. Berkeley, Univ. Calif. Press, 1936.

CALIFORNIA HISTORICAL SOCIETY

Quarterly.

CALIFORNIA LEGISLATURE

Senate and Assembly Journals.

CALIFORNIA SUPREME COURT

Reports of Cases.

CAREY, CHARLES H.

General History of Oregon Prior to 1861. Portland, Metropolitan Press, 1935.

CAUGHEY, JOHN WALTON

California. New York, Prentice-Hall, 1940.

History of the Pacific Coast of North America. Los Angeles, the author, 1933, and New York, Prentice-Hall, 1938.

CLARK, ROBERT CARLTON

History of the Willamette Valley, Oregon. Chicago, S. J. Clarke, 1927.

CLELAND, ROBERT GLASS

History of California, the American Period. New York, The Macmillan Co., 1922.

COWAN, ROBERT ERNEST

Bibliography of the History of California, 1510–1930. San Francisco, John Henry Nash, 1933.

DAVIS, WILLIAM HEATH
  Seventy-five years in California. Edited by Douglas S. Watson.
  San Francisco, John Howell, 1929.
DEWEY, SQUIRE P.
  Bonanza Mines of Nevada; Gross Frauds in the Management
  Exposed; Reply of S. P. Dewey to the Misrepresentations of the
  Bonanza Firms in their Libelous Publication of May 25th, 1878.
  [San Francisco, 1878]
ELDREDGE, ZOETH SKINNER
  The Beginnings of San Francisco, from the Expedition of Anza,
  1774, to the City Charter of April 15, 1850. With biographical
  and other notes. San Francisco, the author, 1912.
  History of California. New York, Century Co., 1915.
FEDERAL WRITERS PROJECT
  California, a Guide to the Golden State. New York, Hastings
  House, 1939.
[FORT SUTTER PAPERS]
  A Transcript of the Fort Sutter Papers, together with the His-
  torical Commentaries Accompanying Them. [Privately printed
  by Edward Eberstadt, 1921]
FULLER, GEORGE W.
  History of the Pacific Northwest. New York, Alfred A. Knopf,
  1931.
GIBBS, GEORGE
  Dictionary of the Chinook Jargon; or, Trade Language of Ore-
  gon. New York, Cramoisy Press, 1863.
HANNA, PHIL TOWNSEND
  California through Four Centuries. A Handbook of Memorable
  Historical Dates. New York, Farrar and Rinehart, 1935.
HARDY, STELLA PICKETT
  Colonial Families of the Southern States of America. A History
  and Genealogy of Colonial Families Who Settled in the Colonies
  Prior to the Revolution. New York, T. A. Wright, 1911.
HISTORY OF SACRAMENTO COUNTY. Oakland, Thompson & West,
  1880.
HITTELL, THEODORE HENRY
  History of California. San Francisco, 1885–97.
HUDSON, FREDERIC
  Journalism in the United States from 1690 to 1872. New York,
  Harper, 1873.
KEMBLE, EDWARD CLEVELAND
  History of California Newspapers, Being a Contemporary Chron-

icle of Early Printing and Publishing on the Pacific Coast. Reprinted for the first time from the Sacramento Daily Union of December 25, 1858. Edited by Douglas C. McMurtrie. New York, Plandome Press, 1927.

Yerba Buena—1846, Sketched through a Loophole. Reproduced from the Sacramento Daily Union of August 26, September 16, and October 14, 1871. With a biographical foreword by Douglas S. Watson. San Francisco, Johnck and Seeger, 1935.

McWILLIAMS, CAREY
Factories in the Field. Boston, Little, Brown & Co., 1939.

NEVINS, ALLAN
Fremont, Pathmarker of the West. New York, Appleton-Century Co., 1939.

NEWSPAPERS
Contemporary dailies and weeklies of San Francisco, Sacramento, Los Angeles, San Diego, Mariposa, Honolulu, Oregon City, etc.

OREGON HISTORICAL SOCIETY
Quarterly.

OREGON PIONEER ASSOCIATION
Transactions.

OREGON SPECTATOR INDEX, 1846–1854
Prepared by the W.P.A. Newspaper Index Project. Portland, 1941.

POWELL, LAWRENCE CLARK
"Flumgudgeon Gazette in 1845 Antedated the Spectator," in Oregon Historical Quarterly, Vol. 41, No. 2, June, 1940.
"Remarkable Contempt Case of Philosopher Pickett," in Interchange Fortnightly, Vol. 1, No. 3, June 28, 1940.
"Western American—An Early California Newspaper," in Papers of the Bibliographical Society of America, Vol. 34, No. 4, 1940.

ROYCE, JOSIAH
California, from the Conquest in 1846 to the Second Vigilance Committee in San Francisco. A Study of American Character. Boston, Houghton Mifflin Co., 1886.

SAGE, RUFUS B.
Rocky Mountain Life; or, Startling Scenes & Perilous Adventures in the Far West. Boston, Wentworth & Lewes & Co., 1857.

SAN FRANCISCO
Great Registers.

SCHERER, JAMES A. B.
The First Forty-Niner, & the Story of the Golden Tea-Caddy.

[Biographical sketch of Samuel Brannan] New York, Minton, Balch & Co., 1925.
Lion of the Vigilantes: William T. Coleman. Indianapolis, Bobbs-Merrill Co., 1939.

SHUCK, OSCAR TULLY
History of the Bench and Bar of California. Los Angeles, The Commercial Printing House, 1901.
The California Scrap-Book. San Francisco, H. H. Bancroft & Co., 1869.

SOCIETY OF CALIFORNIA PIONEERS
Quarterly.

SOULÉ, GIHON, AND NISBET
Annals of San Francisco. New York, Appleton and Co., 1855.

SUTTER, JOHN AUGUSTUS
New Helvetia Diary. A Record of Events Kept by John A. Sutter and His Clerks at New Helvetia, California, from September 9, 1845 to May 25, 1848. San Francisco, The Grabhorn Press for the Society of California Pioneers, 1939.

SWISHER, CARL BRENT
Motivation and Political Technique in the California Constitutional Convention, 1878–79. Claremont, Pomona College, 1930.

TURNBULL, GEORGE S.
History of Oregon Newspapers. Portland, Binfords & Mort, 1939.

VICTOR, FRANCES FULLER
Early Indian Wars of Oregon. Salem, 1894.

VIDETTE, THE
Washington, D.C., 1879–82. Vols. 1–3.

WAGNER, HENRY RAUP
The Plains and the Rockies. A Bibliography of Original Narratives of Travel and Adventure, 1800–1865. Revised and extended by Charles L. Camp. San Francisco, The Grabhorn Press, 1937.

WILLIAMS, MARY FLOYD
History of the San Francisco Committee of Vigilance of 1851. Berkeley, University of California Press, 1921.

WORKS PROGRESS ADMINISTRATION
History of Journalism in San Francisco. Vol. 2, Frontier Journalism. San Francisco, 1939.

YOUNG, JOHN PHILIP
Journalism in California. San Francisco, Chronicle Publishing Co., 1915.

ZOLLINGER, JAMES PETER
Sutter, the Man and His Empire. New York, Oxford University Press, 1939.

Index

CPSIA information can be obtained
at www.ICGtesting.com
Printed in the USA
BVHW040454220922
647590BV00024B/153

9 780520 350168